A PHENOMENOLOGICAL STUDY OF HRM PRACTI

ACQUISITION INTEGRATION PREPARATION: PERSPECTIVES ON

ORGANIZATIONAL CULTURE, HUMAN CAPITAL MANAGEMENT, AND

CHANGE MANAGEMENT

by

Kathryn E. Doseck

STEPHANIE FRASER-BEEKMAN, PhD, Faculty Mentor and Chair

SCOTT FREEHAFER, PhD, Committee Member

GEOFFREY LAENDNER, PhD, Committee Member

William A. Reed, PhD, Acting Dean, School of Business and Technology

A Dissertation Presented in Partial Fulfillment

Of the Requirements for the Degree

Doctor of Philosophy

Capella University

February 2012

UMI Number: 3498080

UMI 3498080

Abstract

This is a phenomenological study that analyzes the integration preparation experiences of human resource management (HRM) professionals in recent mergers and acquisitions between 2008 and 2011. The analysis integration preparation experiences completed for organizational culture, human capital management, and change management. This analysis led to identification of best practices and challenges of integration preparation for HRM professionals. This in turn provided substance, limitations, and direction for future integration preparation research.

Dedication

I am so happy and grateful to reach this point in my educational journey. I would like to thank my savior, Jesus Christ, for His awesomeness and help throughout this journey. I know with all of my heart that You were with me on the long days and nights. Your favor provided me with an amazing committee, participants, and opened the doors that needed to be opened. Thank You. For that reason, I dedicate this dissertation to You.

Acknowledgments

I would like to thank my committee, group administrators, participants, and family. Thank you to Dr. Stephanie Fraser-Beekman, Dr. Scott Freehafer, and Dr. Geoffrey Laendner for the continued support. Even with busy schedules, you made the time to help me become a research practitioner. Your advice, motivation, and follow through helped me push mountains and move beyond my own challenges. Thank you.

A special thanks to the follow administrators of groups on LinkedIn: Dr. Cris Wildermuth with Linked:HR - #1 Human Resources Group; Dave Carhart, MBA, with Human Resources Merger and Acquisition Due Diligence; and Pavel Charney with Post-Merger Integration Professionals. Your willingness and excitement for this study opened the doors for excellent participant recruitment. Thank you.

I am so grateful for the participants' trust, engagement, and the time they spent to share their experiences. These experiences brought clarity, objectivity, and consistency about the research questions. This in turn illustrated the importance integration preparation and/or the lack thereof has on perceived and actual effectiveness of mergers and acquisitions. Thank you.

Lastly, I want to thank my family for their dedication and sacrifice to help me get to this point in my education. You were there through everything. The ups and downs and in between. You respected, encouraged, and most of all showered me with love. I am so grateful. This is the end of an educational journey, but the start to life's new chapter. A chapter that opens a whole other realm of educational lessons and one of which I would not have been able to get to without your support. Thank you.

Table of Contents

Acknowledgments   iv

CHAPTER 1. INTRODUCTION   1

    Introduction   1

    Background of the Study   2

    Statement of the Problem   5

    Purpose of the Study   5

    Rationale   7

    Research Questions   8

    Significance of the Study   9

    Definition of Terms   9

    Assumptions and Limitations   12

    Nature of the Study (or Theoretical/Conceptual Framework)   13

    Organization of the Remainder of the Study   14

CHAPTER 2. LITERATURE REVIEW   15

    Introduction   15

    Organization of Literature Review   15

    Mergers and Acquisitions   16

    Rationale for Mergers and Acquisitions   16

    Types of Mergers and Acquisitions   19

    Merger and Acquisition Challenges   22

    Integration   23

    Integration Preparation   23

Why is Integration Preparation Relevant   24

Integration Preparation Gap Creates Opportunity   25

HRM Integration Best Practices   26

Due Diligence   28

Organizational Culture   29

Human Capital Management   35

Change Management   39

Organizational Change   41

Change Management Principles   41

Methodology and Approach   47

Overall Summary   50

CHAPTER 3. METHODOLOGY   51

Introduction   51

Research Questions   51

Research Design   52

Sample   55

Sampling Frame   56

Sample Methods   57

Participant Selection Criteria   57

Setting   58

Data Collection   58

Data Analysis   62

Validity and Reliability   62

Ethical Considerations   63

CHAPTER 4. RESULTS   65

Introduction   65

Qualitative Research Queries Conducted as Part of Data Analysis   65

Participants   66

Question 1: HR Orientated Integration Preparation Completed   67

Question 2 (a): What Integration Preparation for Organizational Culture?   68

Data Analysis: Organizational Culture Integration Preparation   70

Data Analysis: Limited Organizational Culture Integration Preparation   70

Data Analysis: Comprehensive Organizational Culture Integration Preparation   73

Data Analysis: No Organizational Culture Integration Preparation   80

Conclusion: Organizational Culture Integration Preparation   80

Question 2(b): Integration Preparation for Human Capital Management   81

Data Analysis: Comprehensive Human Capital Management Integration
       Preparation   81
Data Analysis: Limited Human Capital Management Integration Preparation   86

Conclusion: Human Capital Management Integration Preparation   87

Question 2 (c): Integration Preparation for Change Management   87

Data Analysis – Comprehensive Change Management Integration Preparation   88

Data Analysis – Limited Change Management Integration Preparation   91

Conclusion: Change Management Integration Preparation   91

Question 2(d): Were Organizational Culture, Human Capital Management,
       and Change Management Completed Separately or Simultaneously?   92

CHAPTER 5. DISCUSSION, IMPLICATIONS, RECOMMENDATIONS   93

    Research Problem   93

    Relevance and Types of Literature Reviewed   93

    Methodology   93

    Discussion of Study's Findings   94

    Question 1: HR Oriented Integration Preparation Completed   95

    Question 2 (a): Integration Preparation for Organizational Culture   95

    Question 2 (b): Integration Preparation for Human Capital Management   97

    Question 2 (c): Integration Preparation for Change Management   97

    Question 2 (d): Were Organizational Culture, Human Capital Management, and

    Change Management Integration Preparation Completed Separately or

    Simultaneously?   98

    Implications   98

    Implications – Research Question 1   99

    Internal Integration Preparation Team Approach   100

    External Integration Preparation Team Approach   101

    Separate Internal HR Professionals Investigate and Create Integration
        Preparation Plan   101

    Implications Research Question 1: Conclusion   101

    Implications – Research Question 2: How does having an Integration

    Preparation Plan Influence Integration of Organizational Culture,

    Human Capital Management and Change Management throughout
    the process?   102

    Integration Preparation Plan Influences on Organizational Culture Integration 102

Integration Preparation Plan Influences on Human Capital Management

Integration   103

Integration Preparation Plan Influences on Change Management Integration   104

Implications Research Question 2 – Conclusion   104

Limitations   105

Conclusions   106

Recommendations Developed Directly from Data   106

Recommendations for Further Research   109

REFERENCES   111

APPENDIX A. SAMPLE SCREENING QUESTIONNAIRE   118

APPENDIX B. QUALITATIVE CODING SCHEMES   119

APPENDIX C. PARTICIPANT DESCRIPTIVE   120

APPENDIX D. CODING SUMMARY REPORT   121

List of Tables

Table 1. Estimated Time Online Focus Group Interviews   60

Table 2. Participant Attributes   67

Table 3. Participant Attributes Quantified   67

Table 4. Question 2(a) Organizational Culture (OC) Integration   69
Preparation

Table 5. Question 2(b) Human Capital Management (HCM)   81
Integration Preparation

Table 6. Question 2(c) Change Management (CM) Integration   87
Preparation

Table 7. Question 2 (d) Simultaneous or Separate Integration   92
Preparation

List of Figures

Figure 1 – Phenomenological Study of HRM Practitioner M&A Integration
Preparation Conceptual Framework

CHAPTER 1. INTRODUCTION

Introduction

This study investigated the practice of integration preparation for human resource management (HRM) practitioners about organizational culture, human capital management, and change management in mergers and acquisitions. Here, the disjointedness research areas spurred the investigation of how those areas are experienced in integration preparation for HRM practitioners. This study provided academic and industry practitioners with a comprehensive and combined research investigation of HRM integration preparation experiences. The research investigation findings led the researcher to a greater understanding of the research problems. This in turn, presented areas of relevancy within integration preparation for future research and analysis, including recommendations towards an integration preparation framework of organizational culture, human capital management, and change management for HRM practitioners. The intent of this research study was to add to the integration preparation knowledge for HRM practitioners and promote future research in the field.

Background of the Study

Schmidt (2008) noted the importance of HRM practitioner involvement throughout all stages of a merger and acquisition because of the fragile nature of integrating two or more organizations. The fragile nature of mergers and acquisitions is a result of complications of integration of areas of organizational culture, human capital management, and change management (Cartwright & Schoenberg, 2006; Marks & Mirvis, 2010; Schmidt, 2008). These areas have each been identified throughout research as critical success factors of integration in mergers and acquisitions (Cartwright &

1

Schoenberg, 2006; Larsson & Finkelstein, 1999). These critical success factor areas of integration preparation have long been classified within the scope of HRM (Marks & Mirvis, 2010, Schmidt, 2008).

Research has explained and illustrated the importance of understanding these specific critical success factors within integration preparation. For instance, Daimler-Chrysler, Time-Warner and AOL, and Sprint – Nextel each have been recognized as failures as a result of effective planning and integration of the key areas. Lack of integration preparation within these scenarios cost these three companies over $237 billion (Dumon, 2008). Clearly, illustrating that the cost of a lack of integration preparation can add up fast and potentially destroy whatever proposed "strategic" value that brought the organizations into the merger and acquisition in the first place.

Research and analysis of mergers and acquisitions have long shown the importance of integration preparation. researchers such as Argyris, Cartwright, Data, Larsson, Lewin, Kotter, Finklestein, Marks, Mirvis, and Schein have investigated, explored, and authenticated the importance of organizational culture, human capital management, and change management within organizational management. The underlying theory and general implications of these areas are identified as critical success factors to integration of mergers and acquisition. However, the majority of research looks at these areas from an independent perspective of the specific area rather than from a combined integration preparation perspective. Therefore, research has set direction of this study to focus specifically on comprehensive integration preparation for HRM practitioners combining these critical success factors under one appropriate conceptual framework.

2

For instance, research identifies organizational culture as the set norms of an organization that are shaped by the experiences of people within the organization (Cartwright & Schoenberg, 2006; Marks & Mirvis, 2010; Schein, 1985; Schein, 2007; Schmidt, 2008). The shared experiences create the standards, values, and beliefs of doing things within an organization that may vary organization to organization (Schein, 1985). The variance of organizational culture, the combination of two organizations into one organization via a merger or acquisition ultimately brings to surface the issue of accepting, adapting, and/or creating a new organizational culture that is consistent with the objectives and capabilities of the organizations (Badretelli & Bates, 2006; Cartwright, & Cooper, 1993; Marks & Mirvis, 2010; Schmidt, 2008). Research has shown that organizational culture is one of the most significant and overlooked areas within integration preparation (Badretelli & Bates, 2006; Schmidt, 2008). Therefore, this study seeks to identify, analyze, and synthesize organizational culture as it pertains to integration preparation for HRM practitioners.

Human capital management has also been recognized by research as a critical factor within mergers and acquisitions. Often times, it is human capital that brings organizations to the reach a deal (Marks & Mirvis, 2010; Schmidt, 2008). Ironically, human capital management is also frequently noted as a destroyer of value creation (Badretelli & Bates, 2006; Schmidt, 2008). This is because human capital is the talent that actually carries out the objectives (Schiemann, 2006). If there is a lack of integration preparation there is a risk of subpar human capital performance and the overall effectiveness of the merger or acquisition (Schmidt, 2008; Schiemann, 2006). Therefore,

3

this study aims to identify, analyze, and synthesize human capital management as it pertains to integration preparation for HRM practitioners.

Lastly, change management has also been frequently noted as a critical factor within mergers and acquisitions (Marks & Mirvis, 2010). Change management comes into play whenever there is some type of organizational change that is being implemented (Kotter,2005; Lewin, 1947; Schein, 2007). The change in this study is the integration and of two or more organizations. This level of change requires significant understanding, analysis, and application of an appropriate change management approaches. Therefore, the intention of this study is to also identify, analyze, and synthesize core competencies of change management as it pertains to integration preparation for HRM practitioners.

Overall, the proposed research study builds upon research about these critical factors of integration within mergers and acquisitions. However, the route in which this study focuses is in regards to the perspective of integration preparation for HRM practitioners about organizational culture, human capital management, and change management. This study seeks to provide a conceptual framework of these areas that will be relevant to HRM practitioners preparing for integration in mergers and acquisitions. Inspiration for this study resulted from analysis of research of independent areas and the reoccurring theme how these areas influence integration preparation (Larsson & Finklestein, 1999; Marks & Mirvis, 2010; Schmidt, 2008). Research about the critical success areas within integration certainly plays a significant role in the direction of this study because of depth of analysis within the areas. However, just as important is the research about integration preparation for HRM practitioners. The following authors helped to align the need of combination of areas relevant to mergers and acquisitions by

4

breaking down critical factors and the creation of relevant and workable frameworks: Datta (1991), de Haldevang (2009), Larsson & Finklestein (1999), and Schmidt (2008).

Statement of the Problem

The problem of this study is the disconnection of research of integration preparation for HRM practitioners of organizational culture, human capital management, and change management. The perspective of the problem within this study is to focus in on integration preparation of these areas that have shown to individually influence integration value creation and to provide a conceptual connection of these areas. Connecting the disjointedness of these areas will add to and create value to the field of integration preparation of these areas for HRM practitioners. Specifically, this study will potentially impact the effectiveness of integration preparation for HRM practitioners. The potential for HRM practitioners to have a connected conceptual framework for integration preparation may provide greater integration of these areas.

Purpose of the Study

The aforementioned research problem indicates the research "gap" of a comprehensive HRM integration preparation conceptual framework for academic and industry practitioners. This "gap" requires additional research to identify, analyze, and synthesize theory regarding organizational culture, human capital management, and change management of integration preparation for HRM practitioners. This needs to be researched at this time because there is limited information that combines traditional separate theory within a comprehensive integration preparation conceptual framework for HRM practitioners.

5

Furthermore, mergers and acquisitions continue to occur, and they experience up to a 65% failure rate. The critical success factor areas that will be studied and incorporated into a comprehensive conceptual framework for HRM practitioners may provide additional research and insight to integration preparation. With a greater understanding and application of integration preparation of these areas HRM practitioners can build additional value within mergers and acquisitions. Not undertaking this study would impact the development and contribution of knowledge to HRM practitioners within the field of integration preparation.

For instance, over the last 24 months, mergers and acquisitions aggregate spending has increased 32 % from $503.3 billion to $690.1 billion between 2009 and 2010 respectively (Adams & Woo, 2011). From October 2010 to December 2010 nearly $44.5 billion to $58.6 billion was spent on mergers and acquisitions (Adams & Woo, 2011). Indicating a 37.1% growth in aggregate dollar amount of these deals compared to the activities in 2009. The bottom line is organizations are still engaging to mergers and acquisitions to obtain greater financial, operational, and market synergies, however, still face challenges to achieve those synergies.

These challenges often fall into the categories of this research study. Therefore, there is urgency for a comprehensive integration preparation framework for HRM practitioners. This study will provide the researcher with the opportunity to contribute to the existing body of knowledge and open additional areas of inquiry regarding HRM integration preparation. Moreover, scholarly and practitioner journals repeatedly seek out information regarding critical success factors of mergers and acquisitions because of the importance of understanding these factors has on value creation. The topic and context of this research study is relevant to current trends within academic and industry research.

Rationale

Larsson and Finkelstein's (1999) investigated value creation within mergers and acquisitions. The researchers discussed how strategic action in areas including human resource management and organizational theory are paramount to merger or acquisition potential (Larsson & Finklestein, 1999). The premise was that identification, analysis, and application of synergy capabilities in organizations was paramount to the integration process. However, the areas of study were concerned with complementary, synergistic organizational fits. The complementary fits were key to the integration process. However, just as complementary fits are important, understanding non-complementary areas are also essential to the integration process. However, the research focus was on the integration process, not specifically on the preparation of integration. This spurred the rationale of this study to investigate the disconnectedness about integration preparation for HRM practitioners. What research that is available regarding these critical success factors do not look at it from an integration preparation standpoint (Marks & Mirvis, 2010; Schmidt, 2008).

Ideally, before integration actually happens, there must be preparation. This is where this study is different from others is that it takes into account research regarding these critical success areas of integration, but is looking to create a workable, comprehensive integration preparation framework. This study builds upon Larsson and Finklestein (1999) and Schmidt (2008). Neither directly focuses on the topic of integration preparation for HRM practitioners; however, their research frameworks provided value about value creation to the integration process. This dissertation will build upon the theories and concepts regarding integration critical success factors, but from an integration preparation standpoint.

Research has shown these areas as independent influencers, but not on the combination of these areas within the context of a comprehensive integration preparation for HRM practitioners (Barki & Pinsonneault, 2005; Beard & Zuniga, 2006; Chakrabarti, et. al., 2009; Clark, et. al., 2010; Datta, et. al. 1992; MacDonald, 2010; Martin, 2007; Puranam & Chaudhuri, 2009; Shaver, 2006; Stahl & Voight, 2008). These studies revealed the need for integration preparation for HRM practitioners because of their disconnectedness of critical success areas within integration and lack of perspective towards integration preparation. Therefore, the rationale why this research study should proceed is that connected integration preparation will provide HRM practitioners comprehensive understanding of these areas and will focus those areas into an actual integration preparation model.

Research Questions

1. How do HRM practitioners incorporate organizational culture, human capital management, and change management into an integration preparation plan for a merger and acquisition?

2. How does having an integration preparation plan influence the integration of organizational culture, human capital management, and change management throughout the process?

Significance of the Study

This study will provide a valuable contribution specifically within the setting of integration preparation of organizational culture, human capital management, and change management for HRM practitioners and other management practitioners. There is a significant amount of knowledge for practitioners about these areas. However, there is a gap with the incorporation of these areas within integration preparation for HRM practitioners. Therefore, this defined scholarly focus connects research that is relevant to integration preparation for HRM practitioners. Having a comprehensive understanding and approach to these areas within integration preparation will provide HRM practitioners with relevant information about these areas and how to effectively prepare for the pivotal stage of integration.

Definition of Terms

The following terms will be used frequently throughout this dissertation, and for clarification purposes can be defined as:

Acquisition – The purchase of an organization by another organization that will either be incorporated with the acquirer or operate as an independent organization owned by the acquirer (DePamphillis, 2007; DiGeorgio, 2003; Larsson & Finkelstein, 1999; Kale, Singh, & Raman, 2009).

Change management – is the process of effectively identifying, analyzing, and monitoring organizational change. Within the context of this dissertation, the specific areas of change management focus on HRM integration preparation of proposed "new" changes and the change processes (unfreezing, changing, and refreezing) of changes within organizational culture and human capital management (Lewin, 1947; Luscher &

9

Lewis, 2008; Nadler, 1982; Nadler, & Tushman,1999; Ogilvie & Stork, 2003; Schein, 2002; Weick & Quinn, 1999).

Due diligence – Is the fact gathering process that typically occurs prior to a merger and acquisition. The information that is gathered in this process is reviewed to identify the complementary and non-complementary aspects that could influence the performance of the merger and acquisition (DePamphill, 2005; DiGeorgio, 2003; Kale, Singh, & Raman, 2009; McNamara, Haleblain, & Dykes, 2008).

Human capital management – This is much more than just the talent within an organization that carries out organizational activities. Human capital management is about the people side of organizations, and more specifically about following core aspects of organizations such as: recruitment, retention, development, compensation, benefits, and legal(Emmanouilides & Giovanis, 2006; Marks & Vansteenkiste, 2008; Morhman, 2007; Ployhart, Weekley, & Baughman, 2006; Schiemann, 2008).

HRM Consultant – This term refers to a third party subject matter expert that provides HRM professional related services (Caldwell, 2006).

HRM practitioner – This term refers to human resource management practitioners who are professionals within organization that fulfill significant, influential, and strategic roles within organizations (Alvesson & Karreman, 2007; Colbert & Kurucz, 2007; Fairbairn, 2005; Froese, Pak, & Chong, 2008; Lawler & Morhman, 2003; Palthe & Kossek, 2003; Rees & Edwards, 2009).

Integration – Is the unique, complex, and often challenging process of combining two or more organizations during a merger and acquisition. Within the context of this dissertation, the integration processes that will be looked at are organizational culture,

10

human capital management, and change management (Buono, 2005; Cartwright & Schoenberg, 2006; Cording & King, 2008; King, 2007; Kephart, 2010; Kumar, 2009).

Integration preparation –integration preparation is the planning process HRM practitioners explore when identifying, analyzing, and creating specific integration approaches for organizational culture, human capital management, and change management (Chanmugam, Shill, Mann, Ficery, & Pursche, 2005; de Camara & Renjen, 2005; Larsson & Finklestein, 1999).

Merger - The combination of two or more organizations that were previously separate organization, that come together to form a "new" organization (Cartwright & Schoenberg, 2006; DePamphillis, 2007; DiGeorgio, 2003; Larsson & Finkelstein, 1999; Kale, Singh, & Raman, 2009; Kanter, 2009).

Organizational culture – The unique DNA that every organization has that is a result of shared experiences of groups within the organization. The shared experiences create, foster, and maintain the status quo of what is and is not accepted way of doing things within the organization (Hofstedeet al., 2006; Kotter & Heskett, 1992; Schein, 1992; Schein, 1997; Sorensen, 2002). This is the result of the specific values, beliefs, and norms that were established from the shared experiences, and those attitudes and beliefs ultimately shape accepted practices with the organization (Schein, 1992; Schein, 1997; Schein, 2002).

Organizational change - can simply be described as the process of replacing a current system or way of doing things within an organization with a different way that requires the acceptance, implementation, and maintenance of employees within the

11

organization (Argyris, 1997; Feldman, 2000; Jick, 1995; Nadler, 1998; Schein, 2002; Weick & Quinn, 1999).

Assumptions and Limitations

Previous research provided researchers with the opportunity to identify, analyze, and evaluate research for gaps to improve or discredit a particular study. Here, the assumption presented is that there is a disjointed gap between research regarding integration preparation for HRM practitioners about organizational culture, human capital management, and change management. The assumption is that there is a disjointed gap within these areas and that there is a need to bring together these areas into a comprehensive and workable conceptual framework. Doing so would provide a meaningful contribution to HRM academic and industry practitioners about integration preparation of organizational culture, human capital management, and change management in mergers and acquisitions.

Limitations are inevitable, as no particular study is perfect (Richards, 2010). The research objective is to be able to effectively connect disconnected theory about organizational culture, human capital management, and change management with integration preparation. Research within these areas is designed to connect traditionally separated research topics in one combined research study about integration preparation. Limitations of this study include:

- The number of participants.
- The distribution of participants from friendly, hostile, acquired, or acquirer mergers and acquisitions.

- The study may not represent all HRM integration preparation experiences, rather just the experiences of the participants interviewed.

- The information gathered regarding integration preparation may bring additional information not provided within this study into consideration for integration preparation.

- Non-HRM practitioners may also have relevant experiences, know-how, and approaches to integration preparation of mergers and acquisitions, however, this study would not include those perspectives because it is focused only on the perspectives and experiences of HRM practitioners.

Nature of Study

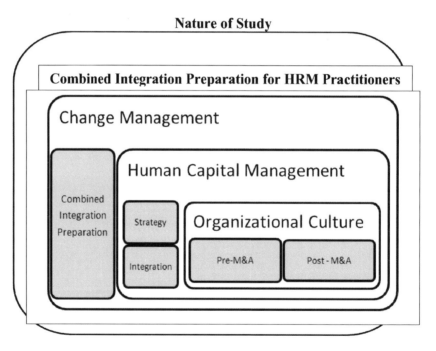

Figure. 1 – Phenomenological Study of HRM Practitioner M&A Integration Preparation Conceptual Framework

Organization of the Remainder of the Study

The next chapter, Chapter 2, is the literature review of past, current, and research regarding the proposed research problems and questions. Specifically, Chapter 2, identifies, describes, and analyzes principles regarding mergers and acquisitions, integration, integration preparation, organizational culture, human capital management, and change management. Chapter 3 presents the methodology aspect of the study, including detailed information regarding research design, sample, setting, instrumentation, data collection, data analysis, validity and reliability, and ethical considerations. Chapter 4 presents the results of the data collection. Chapter 5 goes into more detail about the results of the data collection with an in-depth discussion of the results, implications, and recommendations for future studies.

CHAPTER 2. LITERATURE REVIEW

Introduction

Research provides academic and management practitioners with the opportunity to build upon precedent, analyze relevancy, and create additional research of value that serves to connect disjointed areas within research (Creswell & Miller, 1997). Within this dissertation the focus of the literature review is about creating a greater understanding about mergers and acquisitions, critical factors about integration preparation within areas of organizational culture, human capital, and change management. The objective of this literature review is to build upon research of the aforementioned critical integration preparation factors faced by HRM practitioners in mergers and acquisitions.

Organization of Literature Review

In terms of organization, the literature review will be presented by topical areas: mergers and acquisitions, integration, organizational culture, human capital management, and change management. The topical areas are built upon research in a logical progression of the proposed research questions (Bryant, 2010). This approach to the organization of the literature review helps to present the material in a way that builds understanding and cohesiveness about the topical areas in a way that illustrates the discovery of the gap within the research (Bryant, 2010). Approaching the literature review from this perspective helps to paint the picture of the research problem and move through the discovery of research in the topical areas that opens the door to analysis, synthesis, and application about integration preparation for HRM practitioners in a way to promote greater effectiveness for integration in mergers and acquisitions.

Mergers and Acquisitions (M&A)

In order to move forward with the research problem posed in this dissertation, it is essential to have a clear understanding about the context in which the research problem frequently arises, and that is within mergers and acquisitions. To do this effectively, the following areas about mergers and acquisitions will be discussed: rationale for M&A, types of M&A, recent activity and trends of M&A, and specific challenges of M&A within the context of this dissertation (integration, organizational culture, human capital, and change management). Therefore, by the end of this section, the reader will have a better understanding about mergers and acquisitions.

Rationale for Mergers and Acquisitions

Mergers and acquisitions are the joining of two or more organizations to create a greater combined value than as standalone organizations (Cartwright, 2006; Chakrabarti, Gupta-Mukherjee, & Jayaraman, et. al., 2009). The rational to merge or acquire may vary, however, the logic is to achieve some greater value. Therefore, this section of the literature review will identify the common motivations behind mergers and acquisitions within the context of operational, financial, and market synergies.

Within the context of mergers and acquisitions, synergy is the idea that based on the specific facts and objectives of the organizations involved, that together the organizations would be able to achieve greater results together than alone (DePamphillis, 2007; DiGeorgio, 2003; Kale, et. al., 2009; Larsson & Finklestein, 1999) . This is also known as the 1+1 is greater than 2 or sometimes known as the 1+1 = 3 concept (DePamphillis, 2007). Together the organizations would be more effective together than

16

going at it alone. Further, the value that would be created would also come about in a way that operationally, financially, and market-wise makes more sense.

Operational synergy is composed of many different aspects. The typical operational synergies fall into economies of scale and scope. Within the realm of economies of scale, the reasoning for considering and/or entering a merger and acquisition is about being able to spread the costs associated with operational activities in a way that if together the costs within these areas would be less for the combined organization (DePamphillis, 2007; DiGeorgio, 2003). The reason why the costs would be lower within the context of scale is that one or both organizations may have a much more efficient process than the other, which could ultimately offset the cost through the elimination of redundant positions or entire departments.

On the other hand, economies of scope are related to skills, assets, or other areas that if combined would bring a greater value to the products or services being produced (DePamphillis, 2007; DiGeorgio, 2003). This often includes human capital abilities, technology, and other types of assets that bring significant value to proposition of a merger and acquisition. For example, a recruitment process outsourcing firm may spend a significant amount of money on technology to run its own systems, however, it may decide a merger and acquisition would be more effective with another organization. The other organization looking to merge may have a greater depth of talent, but lack the technology. So, it would be a win-win theory surrounded around economies of scope that rationalizes the purpose behind merging.

Financial synergies that come into play within mergers and acquisitions may come in all shapes and forms. The idea behind the financial impact explored within the synergy will depend on the economic environment and health of the organizations (DePamphillis, 2007; DiGeorgio, 2003). Typically, when there is a positive financial synergy, the organizations involved have something of value to gain from this type of transaction. It could boil down to the cash flows, taxes, debts, equities, and talent. (Leland, 2007). Depending on this situation it may make financial sense to combine organizations in order to achieve greater financial gains and reduce costs.

In addition to operational and financial synergies, market synergy also plays a key role in the rationale in mergers and acquisitions (DePamphillis, 2007; DiGeorgio, 2003; Larsson & Finkelstein, 1999). Market synergy is concerned with several different sub-factors that come into play about the competitiveness, niches, and growth capabilities of the organizations. Theoretically, this concept comes into play when organizations identify areas within the organizations that would be able to be complement one another The complimentary areas would help organizations to create a greater presence within the industry and potential increase the ability to have a greater market share (Cartwright & Schoenberg, 2006; Larsson & Finklestein, 1999). With a greater market share the organizations would be able to effectively achieve more together than as separate organizations.

Organizations contemplating and actually going through a merger and acquisitions may do so for varying reasons; however, traditional factors that come into play in this equation typically surface within operational, financial, and market synergies (Cartwright & Schoenberg, 2006; Chanmugam, Shill, Mann, Ficery, & Pursche, 2005; DePamphillis, 2007; DiGeorgio, 2003; Kumar, 2009) . Whatever the case may be when it comes to the rationale behind mergers and acquisitions, one common theme exists and that is the idea that together the organizations should achieve greater combined value than alone (Cartwright & Schoenberg, 2006).

Types of Mergers & Acquisitions

A merger is commonly referred to as the combination of two or more organizations under the name of one organization (Marks & Mirvis, 2011; Schmidt, 2003). For example, when two or more organizations that combine together via a merger the name of organization will depend on which organization is the "survivor" or the "decedent" (DePamphillis, 2007). The term "survivor" refers to the organization that is formed after the integration. This is typically the case in that of an acquisition, where the organization that acquires another organization does so in a way where the acquired organization now is "controlled" by the acquirer (DePamphillis, 2007; Marks & Mirvis, 2010; Schmidt, 2003). The term "decedent" refers to the organization(s) that is also a part of combination of organizations; however, name of that organization prior to the merger no longer legally exists because the "decedent" organization will go on doing business under the "survivors" name (DePamphillis, 2007).

The type of merger and acquisition should identify specifically which organization is the "decedent" and "survivor". From a legal perspective, there are three different types of mergers and acquisitions: statutory, subsidiary, and equals. Further, from an economic perspective: horizontal, conglomerate, and vertical (DePamphillis, 2007). Depending on the type of merger and acquisition, the process of integration may vary (Cartwright & Schoenberg, 2005; Marks & Mirvis, 2010; DePamphillis, 2007; DiGeorgio, 2007). To effectively build a greater understanding about mergers, these types will be discussed respectively.

19

Within a statutory merger and acquisition, organizations that combine do so in a way that "decedent" organization gives up its previous name and takes on the name of the "survivor" organization. As a result, the "survivor" organization legally is responsible for all of the assets and liabilities of the "decedent" organization (DePamphillis, 2007; Marks & Mirvis, 2010). Further, the "survivor" organization and the "decedent" organization abide to the legal statutes applicable to operation within the state of incorporation of the "survivor" organization. Basically, if the "decedent" organization was originally incorporated in a different state and operated business accordingly within that state, but now merged with an organization that was incorporated in a different state, then the "decedent" organization as result of "death" of its previous organization now operates under "survivor" organization (DePamphillis, 2007).

A subsidiary merger and acquisition on the hand is when an organization that already has the majority ownership of another organization (DePamphillis, 2007; Marks & Mirvis, 2010; Schmidt, 2003). This type of merger can only occur in organizations that actually have a stock that is open for purchase by shareholders (DePamphillis, 2007). Further, the parent organization is the organization that has the primary shareholder ownership in the organization that is greater than the appropriate threshold of ownership. For example, with the state of Delaware the minimum threshold of stock ownership is ownership that is greater than 90% then the parent organization can legally merge with the subsidiary organization without a formal shareholder vote (DePamphillis, 2007).

One type of merger and acquisition that is commonly associated with the technical definition of a merger and acquisition is known as the merger of equals (Cartwright & Schoenberg, 2006; DePamphillis, 2007; Marks & Mirvis, 2010; Schmidt,

2003). Within this type of merger the idea is that two or more organization combine together to achieve a greater synergy together than they would as separate organizations. A greater combined synergy means that the organizations may have a more productive or profitable combined effect than as standalone organizations (DePamphillis, 2007; Marks & Mirvis, 2010).

Contrary to friendly or merger of equals, is a hostile acquisition. A hostile acquisition occurs as a result of an organization purchasing (acquirer) another organization (target) (DePamphillis, 2007). A key difference is that in hostile acquisitions, the target organization's management does not want the acquisition to happen. The perceived threat of the hostile takeover has shown to increase instability of management retention. This is also known as the golden parachute. The golden parachute is known as executive management turnover (Schmidt, 2008). Basically, in all mergers and acquisitions there is the risk of talent leaving the organization, however, in hostile takeovers the risk is greater. The purpose of the acquirer is to achieve greater value, however, the actions to create the value may vary as a result of volatile factors.

In addition to the different legal types of merger, a merger can also be classified differently, for example some of the most common economic perspectives of mergers are either vertical or horizontal (Cartwright & Schoenberg, 2006; DePamphillis, 2007; DiGeorgio, 2007; Marks & Mirvis, 2010) . Depending on the size, type, and industries involved between the organizations plays a role in which classification. A vertical merger happens when two or more organizations merge together; however, because of the differences in the value chains and operational mediums, the organizations merge to create some type of synergy that will produce a greater results in production and/or distribution (DePamphillis, 2007; Marks & Mirvis, 2010). A horizontal merger happens when the organizations involved are within the same industry – similar to the Daimler-Chrysler merger (DiGeorgio, 2007; Marks & Mirvis, 2010).

Depending on the type of merger and acquisition, there may be organizations that combine fully together, which require full integration of the organizations; or there may be acquisitions that have controlling interest in another organization. For the purposes of this dissertation, mergers and acquisitions that fully integrate under one new organization will be studied as a friendly, merger of equals, and hostile. The reasoning behind this selection of mergers and acquisitions is that the gap in research is between integration preparation for HRM practitioners within context of organizational culture, human capital, and change management and to research mergers and acquisitions from the "integration" standpoint it needs to be done with organizations that *actually* integrate two or more organizations together under one organization.

Merger and Acquisition Challenges

The rationale for organizations to actually go through the process of a merger and acquisition is so the combined organizations can create a greater amount of value together than as separate organizations. The logic makes sense if the combined organizations can actually achieve the proposed synergies and do so properly. However, that typically is not the case. In fact, up to 65% of mergers and acquisitions actually fail to achieve the proposed synergies and objectives that brought them to the reach a deal in the first place (Cartwright & Shoenberg, 2006; Chanmugam, Shill, Mann, Ficery, & Pursche, 2005; de Camara & Renjen, 2005; DePamphillis, 2007; DiGeorgio, 2003; Marks & Mirvis, 2011; Schmidt, 2003) . The paradox between organizations moving forward

22

with mergers and acquisitions to achieve more together is limited with high probability of failure (Shaver, 2006; Marks & Mirvis, 2010). Therefore, the remainder of this literature review will focus on the most challenging aspect of mergers and acquisition, which is the integration process.

Integration

The integration stage of a merger and acquisition has been recognized as one of the most crucial stages and can make or break the ability of organizations to actually achieve the planned value creation (Cartwright & Schoenburg, 2006; Cording, et. al., 2008; Kaleet al., 2009; Larsson & Finkelstein, 1999; Larsson & Lubtakin, 2001; Marks & Mirvis, 2011; Swaminathan, et.al., 2008). This section of the literature review will tie together research concerning integration preparation. Specifically, the following areas about integration preparation will be discussed: what it is, why it is relevant, best practices, and the integration preparation areas of this study.

What is integration preparation?

Organizational integration is central to any type of change an organization experiences. Just as there are many different types of change, there are many forms of integration. However, for the purpose of this dissertation, integration is a fundamental stage within a merger and acquisition that actually brings together the organizations that were previously separated. This is the process where the ideas and objectives that have been discussed and put on paper prior to the closing of the deal are actually put into action (Chanmugam, et. al., 2005; Marks & Mirvis, 2010; Schmidt, 2003).

Effective integration is the result of a coordinated effort by management practitioners that have researched, identified, created, and monitored critical factors that

23

could influence the success or demise of the merger and acquisition (Cartwright & Schoenber, 2006; Cording, et. al., 2008; Kale, et. al., 2009; Larsson & Finkelstein, 1999; Marks & Mirvis, 2010). Basically, the integration stage of a merger and acquisition is the stage where the theory and objectives that brought the organizations to the bargaining table to begin with are actually put into action (Marks & Mirvis, 2010). This is also the stage that will illustrate how doable the deal actually is in reality versus the preconceptions of the deal on paper or in meetings.

Research has narrowed the integration stage into a specific process that has several different stages that build upon one another, happen at the same time, and/or are continuous (Cording, et. al., 2008; Kale, Singh, & Raman, 2009; Larsson & Finkelstein, 1999; Marks & Mirvis, 2010). In terms of the "process" of the integration stage theory proposes the following: integration planning, communicating the integration plan, actually creating the "new" integration, developing staffing agendas, integration different organizational functions, and building the "new" organizational culture (DePamphillis, 2007). However, for purposes of this dissertation, the focus is on the traditional first step of the integration process, and that is integration preparation.

Why Integration Preparation is Relevant?

Integration preparation is the concept that in order to actually achieve or at the very least try to achieve the proposed synergies that were behind the rationale for entering a merger and acquisition there needs to be a plan to get the organizations from point A to point B (Chanmugam, et. al., 2005; Marks & Mirvis, 2010). The planning process provides practitioners with the ability to identify and refine any applicable synergy

24

representations, trouble areas that devalue the deal, and how the integration process will be facilitated (Kale, et. al., 2009; Larsson & Finkelstein, 1999; Marks & Mirvis, 2010).

Without adequately addressing and creating a "game plan" for the integration plan itself, the effectiveness of the plan is up in the air (Marks & Mirvis, 2010). The purpose of an integration plan is to set the tone, direction, and expectations of the organizations involved, and more importantly create the right strategies that bring together synergies and handle challenges appropriately (Bardeteli & Bates, 2007; Larsson & Finkelstein, 1999). This is also the stage in the process where the discrepancies or concerns about the terms, promises, and claims of the merger and acquisition are communicated, analyzed, and should be questioned (Cording, et. al., 2008; Kale, et. al. 2009; Marks & Mirvis, 2010).

The Integration Preparation Gap Creates Opportunity

There is significant research that promotes integration planning to operational and financial management professionals, investment bankers, and consultants. These management practitioners certainly bring a significant amount of value to the table for the deal and throughout many stages afterwards; however, there is a gap between the literature and what HRM practitioners do within the integration planning process. The gap is quite puzzling, especially, with research indicating that a significant reason for merger and acquisition failure is the result of "soft" areas that are within the people side of the merger and acquisition, including organizational culture, human capital, and change management (Badratelli & Bates, 2007; DiGeorgio, 2003; Marks & Mirvis, 2010; Schmidt, 2003). These so called "soft" areas related to the people side within organizations are typically areas that within the context of strategic HRM practices.

25

This is not to say that the traditional management professionals commonly associated with integration planning are not familiar nor prepared for those "soft" areas, rather, what is proposed is the addition of HRM practitioners, who have careers that focus on the strategic alignment of these "soft" areas, should be a part of the integration preparation process (Badratelli & Bates, 2007; DiGeorgio, 2003; Marks & Mirvis, 2010). Meaning, HRM practitioners are the business partners of their organizations that focus on dealing with the human capital aspect of their organizations. Because of the scope and nature of HRM practitioners' positions within their organizations under traditional, non-merger and acquisition settings, it is essential for their participation during such time of change. Therefore, the remainder of this section regarding integration will identify, discuss, and analyze theory regarding integration preparation and synthesize the theory regarding the "soft" areas (i.e. organizational culture, human capital, and change management).

HRM Integration Best Practices

Integration preparation should happen before the deal is actually finalized (Chanmugam, et. al., 2005; Schmidt, 2008; Marks & Mirvis, 2010). The information that comes out of the traditional due diligence stage provides valuable information for integration preparation. Traditional due diligence focuses upon information that is considered to be "hard" data based on financial and operational activities (DiGeorgio, 2003; Badrateli & Bates, 2007; Chanmugam,et. al., 2005; Marks & Mirvis, 2010). This information focuses on quantifiable information that illustrates whether or not there is viability financially to proceed with the deal. This information traditionally involves discussions about relevant assets, processes, production, and other areas of synergistic nature. Identifying and understanding traditional "hard" data aspects of organizations before the deal is crucial in determining the plausibility of moving forward with the deal from a financial and operational standpoint, however, it should not be the only areas addressed (Kale et. al., 2009; Marks & Mirvis, 2010).

Within the first stage of integration planning, it is essential that the integration plan is actually put in place before the deal is finalized (Chanmugam, et. al., 2005; Marks & Mirvis, 2010). Having this information already completed and in place before the announcement of the merger and acquisition illustrates that the people involved within the integration plan are on the same page about the integration process and more importantly the fundamental aspects that are laid out within the integration (Barki & Pinsonneault, 2005; Cording, et al, 2008; Kale, et. al., 2009; Marks & Mirvis, 2010; Swaminathan, et, al., 2008). Integration planning and actual discussion of what will and will not be integrated can cause issues; this is where having the right approach to handling these issues before anything is actually finalized is vital to the deal actually being able to come to fruition.

Understanding significant complexities and/or disagreements prior to close of the deal provides the practitioners with the opportunity to see about creating effective resolutions (Chanmugam, et. al., 2005; Cording, et. al., 2008; Marks & Mirvis, 2010). Those resolutions to the challenges must be a part of the integration plan and implemented accordingly. A caveat to this part in integration planning depends on the type of merger and acquisition, i.e. friendly versus hostile and although the plan may be in place, there may be adjustments and/or revisions accordingly (Chanmugam, et. al., 2005; DeCamara & Renjen, 2004; Marks & Mirvis, 2010).

Just as there may be concerns or challenges within the integration preparation

stage, there is significant need to overcome those challenges in a way that is clear,

concise, and addressed to the appropriate audience (Chanmugam, et. al., 2005; de Camara

& Renjen, 2005; Kale, et. al.,2009; Marks & Mirvis, 2010). The integration process can

only be as effective as the preparation and execution of the integration plan which is

created. Integration in mergers and acquisitions is a big part of moving the pendulum

closer to value creation and achievement of the operational, financial, and organizational

goals.

Effective understanding and unity between key challenges of integration is essential

for HRM practitioners to overcome challenges. The challenges frequently cited as

influencers of failure in mergers and acquisitions include: organizational culture, human

capital management, and change management (Cartwright & Schoenberg, 2006; Marks &

Mirvis, 2010). Ironically, these areas are frequently referred to as "soft" areas influencing

mergers and acquisitions because they do not have a "hard" number reflecting a specific

monetary value (DePamphillis, 2003; DiGeorgio, 2005; Marks & Mirvis, 2010).

Although there may not be a specific "hard" monetary value of these specific areas, these

areas certainly can create or destroy value within mergers and acquisitions.

Due Diligence

Before creating an effective integration preparation approach to these underlying

areas influencing organizational value, HRM practitioners should conduct appropriate

due diligence of these areas. Effective due diligence is crucial for the analysis of the

organizations and strengthening the evidence as to whether or not to move forward with

the merger and acquisition (Cartwright & Schoenberg, 2006; Marks & Mirvis, 2010;

Schmidt, 2005). The so called "soft" areas can cause disaster if not adequately identified, analyzed, and synthesized in the due diligence phase (DePamphillis, 2003; Marks & Mirvis, 2010). The areas that will be discussed in this section of the literature review will be organizational culture, human capital, and change management practices. The discussion of theory within these "soft" areas will be presented in the progression of the areas within integration preparation

Organizational Culture

The lack of proper attention, analysis, and synthesis of organizational culture during the due diligence and integration preparation stage can cause significant challenges to the overall viability of mergers and acquisitions (Cartwright & Schoenberg, 2006; Chakarabarti, et. al., 2009; Larsson & Lubatkin, 2001; Marks & Mirvis, 2010). Likewise, having the right amount of information for integration preparation provides HRM practitioners with the relevant and applicable information about organizational culture (Cartwright & Schoenberg, 2006; Marks & Mirvis, 2010). Therefore, this section of the literature review will describe organizational culture, how it is linked to integration preparation, and the value of bridging the gap between integration preparation tailored to finding out about organizational culture and building appropriate integration strategies within integration preparation.

Organizational culture is nothing new to academic and industry practitioners; however, there has been more attention paid to the fundamental aspects of organizational culture and the influences it has over organizational practices and performance (Deal & Kennedy, 1984; Hofstede, et. al., 2006; Kotter & Heskett, 1992; Schein, 1983, 1990, 1995, 1996, 2007). There have been various definitions, perspectives, and meanings

29

surrounding organizational culture. The building blocks of theory and research provides practitioners with extensive opportunities to understand what organizational culture is and the significance it plays in the everyday operations of organizations and in times of change, such as mergers and acquisitions. Overlooking organizational culture theory and taking it at face value would foolishly jeopardize what organizational culture truly is, how it works within an organization, and the influence it has within the integration of organizations in mergers and acquisitions.

The concept of organizational culture as the internal and external genetic makeup of an organization, that, if identified, evaluated, and analyzed, would be able to tell the researcher the so called who, what, where, when, why, and how about the organization. Like DNA in people, no two organizational cultures are alike. Organizational culture can even get right down to influencing both essential and inessential activities that happen within organizations (Schein, 1992; Schein 1997; Schein, 2007). Understanding these unique actions within organizations allows HRM practitioners to connect the organizational cultures' dots. There needs to be research and analysis on areas that have significant differences in cultures that could undermine the deal. Specifically, these organizational culture dots would provide HRM practitioners with the crucial information about accepted and non-accepted actions of organizational culture (Cartwright & Schoenberg, 2006; Marks & Mirvis, 2010; Schein, 2007). With this information, knowing where there are differences and similarities of organizational culture provide HRM practitioners with the valuable information that is used for integration preparation and the overall suitability of a merger and acquisition (Marks & Mirvis, 2010). All of which are essential factors that come into play in identifying the overall compatibility and challenges HRM practitioners may face when integrating organizations.

Just as there are different types of organizations and people that run those organizations, there are different types of organizational cultures. When it comes to analyzing the type of culture, research proposed a three-level approach: observation of organizational artifacts, values, and organizational assumptions (Schein, 1990). From the observation and analysis of these areas HRM practitioners are able to get a better feel about the culture of the proposed organizations in the merger and acquisition. That analysis will ultimately help HRM practitioners be able to put together a tailored integration approach for the organizations in a way that minimizes culture shock.

Part of understanding organizational culture and preventing culture shock is being able to identify and analyze the levels of culture in the organizations. One of the steps HRM practitioners should explore in the due diligence process before the actual integration preparation is observe the actual artifacts of the organizations. Organizational artifacts make up several different aspects within organizations: organizational layout, color, smells, designs, dress code, interaction, communication, procedures, projects, attitudes and accepted behaviors (Schein, 1985; Schein, 1997; Schein, 2003). The experiences shared between members of the organizations can be linked to the actual organizational artifacts. Identifying and understanding the meanings of the artifacts within an organization can help HRM practitioners get a better picture of underlying influences on organizational culture (Cartwright & Schoenberg, 2006; Schein, 2003; Marks & Mirvis, 2010).

31

There is typically significant information about the artifacts within the organization that describes the organizational culture, however, the challenge of ensuring the accuracy of what that actually means may or may not be a certainty (Schein, 1985; Schein, 1990). Artifacts within an organization may provide an indirect or direct indicator about accepted ways of doing things within an organization. However, artifacts do not fully describe explicitly the accepted values of the organization. Schein (1990) stated "we can see and feel that one company is much more formal and bureaucratic than another, but that does not tell us anything about why this is so or what meaning it has to the members," (p.112). This is why identifying and understanding the organizational values that have been shaped by organizational culture is paramount.

Organizational culture boils down to the shared experiences of groups within an organization that ultimately shape organizational values, beliefs, and what is and is not organizational norms (Schein 1983; 1992; 1997). While working together within the organization, groups are linked by experiences and actions that have occurred, whether these actions were directly or indirectly shared, the choices made in particular activities within the organization shaped the values, beliefs, and norms within organizational culture (Schein 1983; Schein, 1992; Schein, 1997). In fact, the values and belief that shape the norm of doing things within the organization is ultimately a result of how these shared experiences manifest with the overall tone that sets the stage for organizational culture based on the social, psychological, and behavioral expectations of actions, inactions, and the general working environment within the organization (Hofstedeet al., 2006; Kotter & Heskett, 1992; Schein, 1992; Schein, 1997; Sorensen, 2002). Culture has legs. Culture is in people and organization. Mismatching culture can cause people to leave the organization.

Organizational culture's influences on mergers and acquisitions is nothing to downplay or ignore (Bardetlli & Bates, 2007). In fact, organizational culture is looked at by practitioners as an influential element that can either destroy or build value in a merger and acquisition. What is meant by destroying or building "value" within a merger and acquisition is how organizational culture can add to or take away from achieving the proposed synergies. Initially the objectives and synergies listed on paper may sound realistic, however, with a lack of due diligence and integration preparation of organizational culture, may limit or destroy the value of the merger and acquisitions. For example, organizational culture differences were cited as the most influential element of the Daimler-Chrysler merger (Bardetlli & Bates, 2007). The differences of the organizational cultures caused a "culture shock" that influenced the integration process and the effectiveness of carrying out objectives.

The concept of organizational culture within mergers and acquisitions is that the new organization is typically a "merger of equals". Meaning that together each organization is equal to the other. As straightforward as "merger of equals" sound, it typically is not the case (Bardetelli & Bates, 2007). Where there are differences, whether minimal or large with organizational culture there is the challenge of integrating the cultures together. That was the challenge of the Daimler-Chrysler merger. The organizational culture of Daimler and Chrysler had their own values, beliefs, and artifacts that shaped the norms of organizational culture (Bardeteli & Bates, 2007; Marks &

33

Mirvis, 2010). Those norms were carried out throughout the organizations – individually, socially, and psychologically.

The Daimler Chrysler merger illustrated the influence organizational culture can pose to overall sustainability and profitability. At face value, the merger made sense between two automobile organizations, however, the internal organizational culture differences proposed the biggest challenge. In fact, within two years of the merger American executives left the company or retired, significant organizational culture clashes continued, and significant financial losses were incurred (Bardeteli & Bates, 2007). So, whether the organizational culture differences are minimal or significant, without the proper amount of due diligence and integration preparation, organizational culture influences the value and viability of a merger and acquisition (Badretelli & Bates, 2007; Cartwright & Schoenberg, 2006; Marks & Mirvis, 2010).

Overall, organizational culture represents the accepted norms of an organization that is a result of shared experiences of members of the organization. These norms are formed by ideas, beliefs, values, and experiences shape the tone of the organizational culture play a huge role in the overall way things function within organizations (Schein, 1997; Marks & Mirvis, 2010). The accepted norms of an organization can be seen directly and indirectly through the social, psychological, and environmental aspects of members and artifacts within the organization (Schein, 1992; Schein, 1993, Schein, 1997). Even small differences between organizational cultures can influence the viability of mergers and acquisitions (Cartwright & Schoenberg, 2006; Chakarabarti, et. al., 2009; Larsson & Lubatkin, 2001; Marks & Mirvis, 2010). Effective due diligence about organizational culture similarities and differences provide HRM practitioners with

34

essential knowledge that can be used to create complementary organizational culture integration strategies. Having a tailored, integration preparation approach to organizational culture provides HRM practitioners with the opportunity to decrease organizational culture incompatibilities which in turn increases viability of organizational culture integration and profitability of the merger and acquisition (Badretelli & Bates, 2007; Cartwright & Schoenberg, 2006; Marks & Mirvis, 2010).

Human Capital Management

Human capital is a critical success factor in a merger and acquisition (Badretelli & Bates, 2007; Cartwright, 1991; Cartwright & Schoenberg, 2006; Chatterjee, et. al., 1992; Puranam, et. al., 2009). First, the people of the organization are what make up the organizational culture that was previously discussed (Hofstedeet al., 2006; Schein, 1990; Schein, 1997; Schein, 2000; Schmidt, 2008). Second, the talented employees are what may lead many organizations to the drawing table for a merger and acquisition (Cartwright, 2006; Marks & Mirvis, 2010). Third, the people are what will ultimately make or break the viability of the merger and acquisition. This is because they are the ones that actually carry out the operational activities of the organization (Badrtalei & Bates; 2007; Cartwright & Schoenberg, 2006; Chatterjee, et. al. 1992; DeGeorgio, 2003; Legare, 1998). Therefore, this section of the literature review will discuss in detail what exactly human capital is, provide specific recommendations about types of approaches to identify and measure human capital within organizations, and lastly, describe why understanding these areas are critical factors that should be included within integration preparation.

35

Human capital is one of the most essential assets to any organization, and often linked to the success or failure in mergers and acquisitions (Badrtalei & Bates, 2007; Chatterjee, et. al., 1992; de Haldevang, 2009; Puranam, et. al., 2009; Schmidt, 2008). Human capital management pertains to the people side of organizations. Specifically human capital management includes: talent recruitment, alignment, capabilities, resources, retention, and turnover (Cartwright, 2006; de Haldevang, 2009; Marks & Mirvis, 2010; Schiemann, 2008). The influential wave of success or failure of a merger and acquisition may fluctuate depending on the level of appropriate attention given to effectively identifying, measuring, and analyzing human capital of organizations prior to integration similar to "the flywheel effect" (Collins, 2009). The "flywheel effect" is the concept that the greater positive momentum of specific actions (in this case, human capital management) causes greater results.

Over up to 65% of mergers and acquisitions fail to achieve the proposed organizational synergies and due so as result of many variables, most notably, variables dealing with human capital (Badrtalei & Bates, 2007; Cartwright, 2006; de Haldevang, 2009; Schmidt, 2008). Measuring, and analyzing human capital. When it boils right down to who, what, where, and when during mergers and acquisitions, it ultimately surrounds the common thread of human capital and if that thread is weak in specific spots or left to fend for itself in certain areas there could be disconnect, or breakage from the overall direction as to where the thread is to be sewn. Ultimately, the thread of human capital, if broken, cannot be stitched according to plan and what remains is error somewhere between organizational strategy, talent capabilities, and engagement.

The concept and theory about the effectiveness of human capital on mergers and acquisitions makes sense. However, actually making use of the appropriate HRM practitioners in the organizations to effectively put together the right level of identification, measurement, and analysis of the new human capital management objectives can be complicated (Badrtaeli & Bates, 2007; Cartwright, 1990; Chatterjee, et. al., 1992; de Haldevang, 2009; Schiemann, 2006). The traditional assumption about the level of influence human capital has on organizational success or failure is transferrable to that of the influence it may have on the organizational strategy of a merger and acquisition (Marks & Mirvis, 2010; Schmidt, 2008). The relevancy and applicability to that of the scenario of merger and acquisition may require some customized "tailoring" of applicable areas and from that customization, additional attention to specific integration preparation strategies that are complimentary and respectful (Marks & Mirvis, 2010; Schiemann, 2006).

The direction and effectiveness of evaluating human capital within the organizations should aim to encompass appropriate analysis of the actual "drivers" of organizational alignment, human capital capabilities, and human capital engagement. Schiemann (2006) noted five distinct areas of "drivers":

1. *HRM systems* – including recruitment, selection, development, and performance management.

2. *IT systems* – information, knowledge, and tools.

3. *Innovation* – ability to create, develop, and maintain an effective cycle of innovation within the organization.

4. *Structure* – actual organizational structure, layout, and functions.

37

5. *Additional unique influencers* – aspects within the organization that make it different than other organizations, i.e. people, competitive advantages, and business processes.

These "drivers" of alignment between organizational strategy, capabilities, and engagement of human capital within an organization are only as influential as the leadership which has created, implemented, and maintains these "drivers" (Schiemann, 2006; Marks & Mirvis, 2010). Ultimately, the representation of organizational strategy and practices influence the overall perception, acceptance, and effectiveness of organizational activities (Badretelli & Bates, 2007). This illustrates the significance human capital at all levels within the organization can have on the overall alignment of organizational strategy, capabilities, and engagement of human capital (Badrtaeli & Bates, 2007; de Haldevang, 2009; Rees & Edwards, 2009; Schiemann, 2006).

Human capital management objectives may change with a merger and acquisition. If there are changes in the human capital management objectives, HRM practitioners are key players to identifying, creating, implementing, and evaluating those changes (Badretelli & Bates, 2007; Deloitte, 2010; Marks & Mirvis, 2010). The Daimler-Chrysler merger illustrated the lack of commitment to human capital management after the merger. There was a significant disconnect and lack of respect for employee involvement, engagement, and growth after the merger. In fact, the inconsistencies of human capital management objectives caused stress, confusion, turnover, and caused significant financial losses (Badretelli & Bates, 2007). Human capital management encompasses all of the relevant systems and processes of organizations to achieve operational and financial objectives (Deloitte, 2010). Having an integration preparation plan that takes into consideration the day to day and strategic aspects of human capital

management is essential to viability and profitability of a merger and acquisition

(Deloitte, 2010; Marks & Mirvis, 2010; Schmidt, 2008).

Overall, human capital management integration preparation in itself is a relevant,

viable, and crucial series of steps for HRM practitioners in mergers and acquisitions

(Chanmugam, et. al., 2005; Cording, et. al., 2008; Deloitte, 2010; Marks & Mirvis, 2010).

Having this information provides HRM practitioners with the ability to "connect the

dots" of strengths, weaknesses, and other areas that could potentially influence the overall

integration performance (Badretelli & Bates, 2007; Deloitte, 2010; Marks & Mirvis). The

strategy that HRM practitioners reap helps to connect the overall alignment of the "new"

organizational strategy with a complimentary integration strategy that will help to yield a

greater overall ability of achieving the sustainable synergies of the merger and

acquisition.

Change Management

The integration process traditionally produces change (Argyris, 1997; Haleblainet

al., 2009; Kotter, 2008; Munner, 2007; Schein, 2002). The idea of combining with

another organization brings concerns and opportunities because the previous way of

doing things is changed and the integration brings uncertainty. This uncertainty may

bring resistance, and resistance can interfere with achieving proposed synergies and

objectives; which can ultimately influence the viability and profitability of the merger

and acquisition.

An integration preparation plan may provide HRM practitioners with change

management practices to effectively manage organizational culture and human capital

39

management integration changes. Academic and industry practitioner research has proven that organizational culture and human capital management can affect the implementation and overall outcomes (Cartwright, 2006; Datta, 1991; Canina & Qingzhong, 2010; Larsson & Finkelstein, 1999; Levin & Gottlieb, 2009; Marks & Mirvis, 2010; Neghab, et. al., 2009). It is reasonable to connect that if both organizational culture and human capital management factors can influence the performance of the merger and acquisitions, that there should also be an integration preparation approach for change management within these areas. Therefore, this section of the literature review will discuss organizational change, change management practices, and lastly, tie together this information in a way that encompasses the relevancy and imperative nature of incorporation with integration preparation.

In order to effectively understand organizational change and change management techniques, it is essential for HRM practitioners to be familiar with accepted principles and theories regarding change. By understanding the theoretical and application oriented approaches to organizational change and change management, HRM practitioners will be more effective at tailoring a strategic integration preparation approach that is complementary to the "new" organizational changes and strategy. This provides HRM practitioners to learn more about organizational change and change management, but to link theory with creation of effective strategy that will help increase the probability of effective performance within organizational culture and human capital management integration.

Organizational Change

Organizational change is the process of replacing a current system or way of doing things within an organization. The change requires acceptance, implementation, and maintenance (Argyris, 1997; Feldman, 2000; Jick, 1995; Kotter, 2005; Nadler, 1998; Schein, 2002; Weick & Quinn, 1999). Within the context of a merger and acquisition, changing what employees have done for quite some time and accepting something new can be a profound challenge. Depending on the specific circumstances and objectives, the merger and acquisition may require minimal, incremental, or radical change. Although there may be different types of proposed changes, there still is the need for familiarity and understanding about change management principles, and how these principles may tie into the creation of an effective integration preparation plan.

Change Management Principles

Change happens all of the time within organizations. The stages of change include: birth, growth, development, decline, and death (Burnes, 2004; Lewin, 1947; Nadler, 1982; Schein, 2002). There may be minimal, incremental, and/or radical changes that may come into play with organizational culture and human capital management in mergers and acquisitions. Organizational culture and human capital management are in themselves two areas that encompass many subsystems that shape the way organizations do business (Schiemann, 2006; Schein, 2007; Schein, Goffee, & Jones, 1997). Integrating two organizations that have differences within these areas requires a careful understanding of change management practices (DiGeorgio, 2001; DiGeorgio, 2003; Larsson & Finkelson, 1999; Schiemann, 2006; Smollan & Sayers, 2009; Sorenson, McEvily, Ren, & Roy, 2006).

41

In order for effective change management to actually happen there needs to be a cohesive understanding about areas within the "new" organization that will be changing and how those changes may ultimately influence organizational culture and human capital management (Munner, 2007; Nadler, 1982; Nadler, 1999; Schein, 1999; Schein, 2002; Smollan & Sayers, 2009; Van Dijk & Van Dick, 2009). This research and analysis of the current systems within the organizations is also referred to as the Diagnostic Principle of Change Management (Feldman, 2000; Nadler & Tushman,1989; Nadler & Tushman, 1999; Schein, 2002; Weick & Quinn, 1999). What this means within the context of organizational culture and human capital management is that HRM practitioners need to be aware of similarities and differences between the organizations. This could ultimately influence the viability of change and performance of the merger and acquisition. Having this understanding will provide HRM practitioners with opportunities to tailor the right approach to create a change management strategy that will help to actually make the proposed changes happen. (Feldman, 2000; Fiol & Lyles, 1985; Jick, 2001; Schein, 2002; Weick & Quinn, 1999).

Building upon the Diagnostic Principle is understanding the different stages of change. This is especially the case for HRM practitioners because it reminds practitioners that every action regarding current and proposed change is somewhere within the change cycle, and that the actions designed to change the current system, must include the right amount of "force" to change the current system. This change management principle is known as the Quasi-Stationary Equilibrium of Multiple Forces (Burnes, 2004; Lewin, 1947; Nadler, 1982; Schein, 2002). The reasoning behind this theory is that because there is always some level of change happening within any system in an organization, it is essential to understand what forces, such as activities, are occurring that keep that system up and running.

The information about forces influencing organizational culture and human capital should be identified, analyzed, and evaluated (DiGeorgio, 2003; Munner, 2007; Neghab, Sardari, & Imani, 2009; Paine, 1984; Schein, 2002; Schiemann, 2006). This information will provide HRM practitioners with specific indicators where there are minimal, incremental, or significant differences between organizational culture and human capital management (Allred, Boal, & Holestein; 2010; Badrtalei & Bates, 2007; Clark, Gioia, Ketchen, David, Thomas, 2010; Fairbairn, 2005; Hofsteade, Neujen, Obhayv, Sanders, Arnold, & Spell, 2006; Kendra & Taplin, 2004; Knodel, 2004; Lawler & Mohrman, 2003; Levin & Gottlieb, 2009; MacDonald, 2010; Mohrman, 2007; Schiemann, 2006). The evaluation of how these areas are currently used and what changes may need to occur is paramount to change preparation.

After the actual diagnosis, evaluation, and creation of the "new" proposed forces that will be implemented to move from the current way of doing things is the process of actually pull together a plan that addresses the preparation. (Nadler & Tushman, 1989; Lewin, 1947; Schein, 2002). The preparation of implementation should focus on the three specific phases of change that must occur in order for change to actually to shape: unfreezing, implementing, and refreezing (Lewin, 1947; Nadler & Tushman, 1989; Schein, 2002; Weick & Quinn, 1999).

One of the most difficult phases of change management is the initial unfreezing stage (Schein, 2002). The principle behind the unfreezing stage is that it requires some sort of motivation or reasoning about why the current system should be replaced with another. Basically, HRM practitioners need to create a level of discomfort about the current organizational culture and human capital management systems that need to change and the reasoning behind those changes. To do this, HRM practitioners will need to show how the current organizational culture and/or human capital management systems are not fully conducive to the "new" organizational culture and human capital management strategies (Cartwright, 1993; Chatman & Eunyoung, 2003; Datta, 1991; Eriksson & Sundgren, 2005; Fairbain, 2005; Fawcett, Brau, Rhoads, Whitlark, & Fawcett, 2008; Smollan & Sayers, 2009). Keep in mind, that every organization and every merger or acquisition is going to be different. so within these two areas, the changes may be minute, subtle, or radical. Depending of the actual proposed changes, the approach to "unfreezing" the current organizational culture and human capital management systems may be different.

Whatever the case is in regards to level or type of change that must occur, it is essential that HRM practitioners create and communicate the reasoning behind why the current system is not helping to achieve full organizational capabilities (Argyris, 1997; Lawler & Mohrman, 2000; Lewin, 1947; Schein, 2002; Weick & Quinn, 1999). It is essential that communication is respectful to the current systems and participants. This illustrates the urgency of moving forward with better systems that are in better alignment with the "new" organization (Feldman, 2000; Kotter, 2005; Schein, 2002; Smollan & Sayers, 2009; Wan, 2008; Weick & Quinn, 1999). Doing so may help HRM practitioners build a case behind the reasons for the proposed changes.

HRM practitioners have the challenge and opportunity of creating an effective change management strategy that illustrates the importance, reasoning, and urgency for the proposed changes. The objective for HRM practitioners in this phase is to do so in a way that does not tear apart or disrespect the past or current way of doing things, but brings the change recipients to an understanding and acceptance of the proposed changes in a way that links clarity, concern, and consistency about the reasons to move forward with the prospective changes and how those changes will help to move the organization in a more successful direction (Jick, 2001; Kotter, 2005; Nadler & Tushman, 1989; Nadler & Tushman, 1999; Schein, 2002; Smollan & Sayers, 2009; Weick & Quinn, 1999). Creating the understanding, connection, and vision for the new changes is part of the Energy Principle. The idea behind the Energy Principle is that the reasoning of the new changes should create the acceptance, motivation, and energy needed to implement the new changes (Feldman, 2000; Lord, et. al., 1999; Nadler & Tushman, 1989; Weick & Quinn, 1999). Because most people resist change, there needs to be vision, motivation, and acceptance of change.

Once HRM practitioners have created the discomfort with the current system or approaches for organizational culture and human capital management, and built reasoning for the proposed changes, the next stage of the change management process is implementing the changes (Lewin, 1947; Schein, 2002). This part of the change management process will encompass new concepts, meanings, and ways of doing things within the "new" organization. Schein (2002) noted "if the change is a simple behavior one, people make the change, however, with complex attitudinal change or changes shared in basic assumptions (culture), there is the additional problem that the change targets may initially not even understand the "new" attitude or assumption," (p.38). Here, within the context of dealing with organizational culture and human capital management,

45

there is a greater need for clarification, consistency, and understanding of the "new" changes that influence the "attitudes or assumptions" about doing things (Allred, Boal, & Holestein; 2010; Clark, et. al., 2010; Levin & Gottlieb, 2009; Nadler & Tushman, 1989; Neghab, et.al, 2009). So, within these types of changes there needs to be a strategy in place to signal, psychologically and behaviorally the "new" organizational culture and human capital management way of doing things in a way that cognitively supplements previous assumptions and attitudes (Schein, 2002).

Lastly, the final phase of the change management process is the refreezing stage (Schein, 2002). During this stage, the new systems, attitudes, assumptions, and behaviors regarding organizational culture and human capital management are internalized. In order for this refreezing process to last, these behaviors about organizational culture and human capital management must actually fit with the overall organization (Levin & Gottlieb, 2009; Schein, 2002; Schiemann, 2006). Otherwise, the new changes which have been implemented and seems to be going well could revert back to the previous attitudes, assumptions, and behaviors regarding organizational culture and human capital management. A rewards system to promote the success of the change may also be helpful for the new changes to take hold to the system. So, the key for HRM practitioners to remember with managing effective change in these areas is creating the best types of changes within these areas that actually fit with the organizations and establishing a rewards system.

In all, HRM practitioners when faced with integration of two or more organizations in a merger and acquisition may be challenged to create an effective strategy that aligns the "new" organizational goals within these areas, but this new

46

strategy could be different to the organizations. Even the smallest changes within organizational culture and human capital management systems can influence the performance of a merger and acquisition (Cartwright, 2006; Fairbairn, 2005; Higgins & McAllister, 2004; Schein, 2002; Schiemann, 2006; Wan, 2008). Therefore, it is crucial for HRM practitioners to be familiar with organizational change, change management principles, and more importantly create the most effective, tailored change management integration preparation plan that is conducive to the organizations. Doing so, helps to harness the ability and viability of sustainable change that will ultimately be an influencer on the overall key areas where change is being implemented within mergers and acquisitions.

Methodology and Approach

Larsson and Finkelstein (1999) used a case study approach to analyze human resource management issues influencing value creation in mergers and acquisitions. The study had profound influence on research of human resource management aspects of mergers and acquisitions. Further, their 1999 study that have been cited by hundreds of peer-reviewed scholarly and industry practitioner authors current research has opened more research opportunities regarding HRM in mergers and acquisitions. It was this study that initially spurred this researcher's interest in the research of the questions in the proposal. Therefore, the remainder of this section of the literature review will address the following areas: selection, support, and reasoning of methodology and approach.

Methodology selection is crucial to the effectiveness of this research study. The methodology selected for this study is a phenomenological. Phenomenological approach allows the researcher to investigate shared experiences, attitudes, and understandings

47

about a particular phenomenon (Hendry, Pringle, & McLafferty, 2011). This approach allows the researcher to investigate with participants that have actually experienced the phenomena in question. Husserel (1994) noted that this approach used those direct experiences of participants and those experiences bring reflective value to understanding the phenomena.

In addition, a phenomenological approach is strongly supported because of the use of epoche. Epoche is the reduction of researcher bias (Hendry, Pringle, & McLafferty, 2011; Husserel, 1994). The reduction of personal bias occurs because the study is focused on the actual experiences of participants of the phenomena and not the perception of what the researcher has about the phenomena. Husserel (1994) pointed out that "phenomena" includes anything that participant has consciously experienced. This means that the participants must actually have primary experience and would be able to report specific detail about that experience (Bradbury-Jones, Irvine, & Sambrook, 2009; Hendry, Pringle, & McLafferty, 2011).

The phenomenological approach allows the researcher to let go of any biases or preconceived ideas about a phenomena and accept the organic flow of detail from participants' experiences (Bradbury-Jones, Irvine, & Sambrook, 2009; Hendry, Pringle, & McLafferty, 2011).In turn, this allows the researcher to be open to meanings that flow from the data collected and let that data set the terms of the investigation (Capella University, 2011).

The phenomenological approach has six commonly referred to steps to ensure consistency and validity:

    1. Incorporation of epoche,

2. Elimination of personal biases replaced with free-flowing open-ended experiences to qualitative interview questions asked to participants,

3. Analysis of experiences to reach a greater understanding of shared experiences of the phenomena,

4. Analysis to understand to create meaning "units" of experiences

5. Synthesize the meaningful "units" to gain a deeper psychological understanding of participants' experiences,

6. Final synthesis of participants' experiences into overall summary that describes phenomena being studied

(Capella University, 2011; Hendry, Pringle, & McLafferty, 2011; Husserel, 1994). These steps within the phenomenological approach allow the researcher to systematically approach the organic process of the investigation. This ensures that the participants' experiences are accurately collected, analyzed, and synthesized to reflect the actual phenomena.

Within this study the research investigated HRM integration preparation. The objective of using this methodology allowed the researcher to achieve a better understanding of these phenomenons. The richness of the experiences participants provided to researcher allowed the researcher to investigate deeper into structures of approaches used to integration preparation. The quantitative nature of Larsson and Finklestein's study brought great value to the academic and practitioner community (Larsson & Finklestein, 1999). Their paramount study of HRM issues influenced value creation in mergers and acquisition spurred the research quest for more detail about integration preparation of these areas. Using the phenomenological approach allowed the

49

researcher to have a greater understanding about participants' actual experience regarding integration preparation. These experiences helped the researcher address the research questions of this study, reach appropriate findings, and discuss future research opportunities of integration preparation for HRM practitioners.

Overall Summary

Organizational culture, human capital management and change management have been recognized as contributors to value creation of mergers and acquisitions, but up to 65% of mergers and acquisitions fail to achieve operational and financial synergies (Cartwright & Schoenberg, 2006; Larsson & Finkelstein, 1999; Marks & Mirvis, 2010). These areas are influencers to such high failure rates. Inadequate integration preparation of these areas value creation is limited and in most cases, destroyed value (Bardeteli & Bates, 2007; Cartwright & Schoenberg, 2006; Marks & Mirvis, 2010). Each of these areas has been covered extensively by researchers separately, leaving a gap in research about integration preparation of these areas combined.

The disjointedness of integration preparation for HRM practitioners has led to this study. Researchers have shown these areas to be influences of value creation; however, in terms of integration preparation of these combined areas for HRM practitioners the research is limited. Furthermore, the level of detail and depth into actual HRM practitioners' experiences within integration preparation is limited. For that reason, further phenomenological investigation of HRM practitioners' experiences within integration preparation was studied in this dissertation. This provided a greater understanding to integration preparation and promotes future research opportunities about integration preparation.

CHAPTER 3. METHODOLOGY

Introduction

Integration preparation of organizational culture, human capital management, and change management during mergers and acquisitions requires in-depth research about the actual experiences of HRM practitioners. The reason for this is because HRM practitioners are the people within their organizations that traditionally oversee these areas of their organizations. These areas are pivotal factors influencing value creation or destruction of a merger and acquisition. Using a research methodology that captures information addressed in the research questions of this study provides the researcher a high quality of richness about the actual practical creation and application of integration preparation of organizational culture, human capital management, and change management.

The purpose of this research study was to investigate integration preparation of organizational culture, human capital management, and change management. The disjointed nature of the research influences the practicality of integration preparation of these areas for HRM practitioners. Further, as research showed, these areas separately influenced the value creation of mergers and acquisitions. This study investigated the challenges and strengths of these areas within integration preparation. This confirmed and opened new discussion of disjointedness within integration preparation.

Research Questions

To get a better understanding about integration preparation experiences, HRM practitioners were asked the following research questions:

1. Was there any integration preparation completed? Yes or No?

2. What integration preparation was done for organizational culture, human capital management, and change management? Were these areas done separately or simultaneously?

3. How did integration preparation or the lack thereof influence the integration of the acquired or merged companies?

Research Design

Richards (2010) noted that the research design for a qualitative study should be complementary to the overall objectives of the research questions. The research questions within this study were concerned with investigating the experiences and perceptions of integration preparation of organizational culture, human capital management, and change management of those areas by HRM practitioners in mergers and acquisitions. This information provided an in-depth analysis of actual experiences to integration preparation. Therefore, the research design used the phenomenological approach.

A phenomenological qualitative study is designed to examine the actual experiences from the participants' point of view of those experiences (Creswell, 2003; Richards, 2010; Robinson, 2011). This approach provided the researcher with relevant information that addressed and answered the research questions of this study. The reason for this methodology was the relevant and consistent approach for this study was because the phenomenological approach concentrates on the experiences of participants (Giorgi, 2002; Hendry, Pringle, & McLafferty, 2011; Moustakas, 1994). The experiences in exploration of this study were the research questions of this study.

Investigating the phenomena, allowed the researcher to learn more about the experiences (Bradbury-Jones, Sambrook, and Irvine, 2008). The nature of the

52

phenomenological approach allowed the researcher to gather relevant and applicable information to research questions that address the specific phenomena. Husserl (1965) as cited by Moustakas (1994) noted that the data collected from this approach was the result of personal experiences and that those experiences that are shared consciousness and non-biased. Here, within this study the phenomena focus was specifically within the research questions and concerned with the integration preparation experiences of HRM practitioners.

Using the phenomenological approach provided the researchers with an objective approach of understand the subjective experiences of HRM practitioners (Moustakas, 1994). Here, the research problem was the research disconnect of integration preparation of organizational culture, human capital management, and change management of these areas for HRM practitioners in mergers and acquisitions. The research approach used to gain phenomenological qualitative data was focus group interviews (Bradbury-Jones, Irvine, & Sambrook, 2009; Hendry, Pringle, & McLafferty, 2011; Robinson, 2011).

Focus group interviews provided the researcher with the approach to collect phenomenological experiences from participants that are directly applicable to the research questions (Bradbury-Jones, Irvine, & Sambrook, 2009; Richards, 2010). The focus group methodology provided the researcher with a forum to purposefully collect data from participants from a shared community (Krueger & Casey, 2008; Morgan, 1996). The shared community served HRM practitioners who have gone through a merger and acquisition between 2008 and 2011. This shared community served to provide a comprehensive understanding of about the phenomenological experiences of

53

the research questions. This was relevant information which was used to create a conceptual integration framework and potentially address areas of future research.

Focus group interviews provided enriched the data collection because of participant interaction, reflection, and clarification of experiences among participants (Bradbury-Jones, Sambrook, & Irvine, 2008). Moreover, these interactions helped to provide an organic flow of experiences that incorporates a descriptive understanding of experiences to the phenomena that was studied (Cote-Arsenault & Morrison-Beedy, 2001). An argument against the use of focus group interviews within a phenomenological study is that the group discussion and interaction would reflect the group members' experiences and takeaway from the actual individual participant experiences to the phenomena (Webb & Kevern, 2001). Phenomenological research at its core is about individual experiences of phenomena (Bradbury-Jones, Sambrook, & Irvine, 2008). Therefore, critics to the use of focus group interview in collecting data argue that group collaboration is not a true phenomenological reflection of individual experiences, rather a compromised reflection (Webb & Kevern, 2001). Critics argued the phenomenological research is compromised by reflection and discussion of the groups' experiences.

However, research indicates that focus group interviews promote cross-checking, clarification, interaction, and depth of understanding of the phenomena being studied (Bradbury-Jones, Sambrook, & Irvine, 2008). Focus group interviews did not overlook individual experiences. Rather, by design, focus group interviews brought participants together within a setting and discussed the particular questions individually. Sorrell and Redmond (1995), as cited by Bradbury-Jones, Sambrook, and Irvine (2008) noted that participants of focus group interviews should be able to share his or her "narrative as a

54

self-contained story with minimal interruptions and then members of the group can add valuable perspectives as the story unfolds, probing for more information and adding their own insights related to shared meanings" (p.669). Individual reflection and interaction is not undermined, but is the core of focus group interviews which builds upon those experiences with deeper discussion and reflection.

Ultimately, the objective of the research design of this study was to gain a greater descriptive and interpretive understanding of the phenomena being studied based on participants' individual experiences. From these experiences, the dialogue, reflection, and group collaboration aspect of focus group interviews also provides greater clarification, double-checking, and understanding of the experiences of the phenomena from an individual participant basis (Bradbury-Jones, Sambrook, & Irvine, 2008). Bradbury-Jones, Sambrook, and Irvine (2008) stated "in our experiences, focus groups enhance rather than compromise phenomenological research" (p. 668). Using a focus group interview approach allowed the researcher to gain a deeper understanding of these experiences through participant discussion, reflection, and collaboration of experiences.

Sample

The target population for this study is HRM practitioners who have gone through a merger and acquisition between 2008 and 2011. The reason to select HRM practitioners who have actually gone through recent merger and acquisition is because this study was concerned with understanding more about the experiences of integration preparation. The integration preparation focus was about organizational culture, human capital management, and change management. The HRM practitioner population provides a greater understanding of the experiences and knowledge of integration preparation within

55

these areas because these areas are within the scope of HRM (Cartwright & Schoenberg, 2003; Marks & Mirvis, 2010; Schmidt, 2008). Doing so, would provide the researcher with a greater understanding of critical factors influencing integration preparation of these areas. This would provide valuable information to assemble these factors into a workable conceptual integration preparation framework.

Sampling Frame

Krueger and Casey (2000) noted that the traditional study that uses a focus group approach should have roughly six to twelve groups within the same community. The quantity of participants per student may vary depending on the expectations of the study. The expectations of the study include: purpose of the study, information needed to be gathered, and qualifications of participants (Krueger and Casey, 2000). The objective is of using focus group methodology as a sampling frame is to get enough information from participants about the research questions. This is known as "theoretical saturation" that shows patterns from participant responses (Krueger and Casey, 2000).

Here, within this study the community that is referred to is HRM practitioners who have undergone a merger and acquisition between 2008 and 2011. So, the sampling frame used five focus groups, with a total thirteen qualified participants. Eighteen participants initially participated in the study, but five were considered unqualified because of participant criteria (Creswell & Miller, 1997; Creswell, 2003; Huberman, 2002). The actual sampling methods used in this study included reaching out to prospective participants via social media networks, LinkedIn via HRM professional affiliation online communities.

56

Sample Methods

Social network communities via LinkedIn included: Post-Merger Integration
Professionals, Human Resources Merger and Acquisitions Due Diligence, and LinkedHR
that have a combined professional membership of 447,551 people. An initial discussion
thread about the background, purpose, research questions, and focus group interaction
was posted within the online communities' discussion forums to voluntarily recruit
participants within those communities.

Participant Selection Criteria

In order to achieve valid consensus and understanding of the research questions, and
moderate effective focus group interviews, criteria were created to ensure that
participants were actual HRM practitioners at the time of the merger and acquisition.
Further, experience and education background were also criteria factors for participants,
requiring at least two years of applicable HRM experience (Management, Director,
and/or Executive HRM practitioners at the time of the M&A) and at least a bachelor's
degree in a HRM or Business related field. This criterion helped to solidify the
"community" of the participants which ultimately provided more meaningful data for the
research questions in this study (Bradbury-Jones, Irvine, & Sambrook, 2009; Creswell &
Miller, 2000; Greenbaum, 2000; Huberman, 2002; Krueger & Casey, 2008; Richards,
2010). Lastly, this sampling strategy has also been referred to as structurational.
Meaning, where the subjects that are selected for research are purposefully selected based
on specific knowledge and experience that provides descriptive discourse in a research
study (Huberman, 2002; Miles & Huberman, 1994; Morgan & Smirich, 1980; Richards,
2010).

Setting

The setting of the focus group interviews took place via the web conferencing host GoToMeeting.com. The online web conferencing provided a safe, secure, and easy to access environment for participants to collaborate and participate with the structured interview questions.

Data Collection

Data collection included: a two to five minute online pre-screening recruitment questionnaire, participant completion and return of informed consent form to the researcher, Appendix A, and one, sixty minute online focus group interview. The researcher initiated initial communication with prospective participants was via LinkedIn discussion forums thread in professional affiliations community boards. The initial thread was used as recruitment tool to present the background of the research study, purpose of the study, type of study, and asked for voluntary participants with the appropriate experience. Prospective participants responded to the thread via LinkedIn email and/or telephone to the researcher.

Interested participants completed a brief, two to five minute online pre-screening questionnaire via a survey link that was embedded within the recruitment posting. Participants that met the criteria in Appendix A, and selected to participate were contacted by the researcher. The researcher emailed the Informed Consent Form to the prospective participants. Participants reviewed, signed, and returned the completed Informed Consent Form to the researcher via email before the actual participation of the focus group interview.

Once the completed and signed Informed Consent Form was received, the researcher scheduled the online focus group interviews. Participants selected the time that worked best with their schedules (Creswell & Miller, 2000; Greenbaum, 2000; Krueger & Casey, 2008; Richards, 2010). The researcher emailed confirmation of their acceptance of attending a focus group interview.

The actual interaction for the focus group interviews used the telephone and/or computer interaction. Participants had the options to login to the meeting by using their computers or to call a toll-free, fully integrated conference line. Structured interview questions created by the researcher were presented to participants during this interaction. To help increase productivity of the focus groups interviews, the researcher also emailed the questions upon confirmation of participation to the participants (Bradbury-Jones, Sambrook, & Irvine, 2008). This allowed participants the opportunity to review and prepare their responses in advance and perhaps influenced the quality of the responses provided within the focus group interview (Krueger & Casey, 2000). Preparation prior to the focus group interview was optional, however, participants that select to do so, may have spent an estimated ten to thirty minutes preparing their responses. This however, may have varied depending on individual circumstances of participants.

The researcher facilitated the focus group interviews accordingly. The researcher conducted eight focus group interviews via online web conferencing tool, which were more than the researcher had anticipated www.GoToMeeting.com. Each focus group interview had one to three participants, which was less than the researcher had anticipated. The focused group interviews ranged from thirty to sixty minutes. The variance in time depended on the number of participants per interview, readiness of their

59

responses, and overall interaction. The researcher asked three structured interview questions tailored to the research questions of the study (Creswell, 2003; Greenbaum, 2000; Huberman, 1984; Miles & Huberman, 1994; Huberman, 2002; Sealeet al., 2004). Structuring the questions in a way that captures the information regarding the research questions of this study is essential; however, just as important is ensuring clarity of the questions and the timeframe needed to adequately allow participants to answer the questions. Research has shown that questions that are too complex or too simple can influence the responses of participants (Creswell, 2003; Miles & Huberman, 1994; Seale, et., al., 2004; Richards, 2010).

The researcher asked three structured interview questions during the focus group interview. Table I illustrates the estimated time of completion for the online focus group interviews. The estimated timeframes were a result of average time for participants to answer the interview questions. Depending on the number of participants the times varied. It also noteworthy, some participants took more or less time to answer the interview questions.

Table 1. Estimated Time for Online Focus Group Interviews

Interview questions	One participant	Two participants	Three participants
Question 1	> 10 seconds	> 20 seconds	> 30 seconds
Question 2	10 - 15 minutes	20 - 30 minutes	40 – 60 minutes
Question 3	3 – 4 minutes	6 – 8 minutes	9 – 12 minutes
Total time	13 – 20 minutes	27 – 40 minutes	50 – 72 minutes

Although there is no standard quantity of time per participant in a focus group interview, the objective is to provide the participant with adequate time to think,

60

respond, and collaborate with other participants (Bradbury-Jones, Sambrook, & Irvine, 2008). However, at the same time, the questions asked should be clear, concise, and not overwhelming to the participants (Krueger & Casey, 2003; Richards, 2010). The goal is to provide questions that are relevant to the research study, but, not too complex or time consuming. This helped to promote quality, structure, relevancy, and clarity for participants. Furthermore, it is respectful to participation, time, and interaction within the focus group (Richards, 2010).

The focus group interviews were digitally recorded by the hosting website, GoToMeeting.com. This recording served as a direct, unbiased, and secure form of keeping track of the communications that occurred within the meeting, including the participants who joined the meeting, and how long the meeting lasted. This information is accessible to the researcher, who is the moderator of the interview. Further the recordings of the focus group interviews were digitally transcribed using Dragon® Speech Recognition Software. To ensure accuracy the digital transcription will also be reviewed by the researcher. The digital transcription of the audio recording provided an unbiased, accurate, and secure transcription of the focus group interviews. The recording of non-verbal communication, such as messaging, during the web conference call, was transcribed by the researcher, and the original messages accessible via the conference call archive.

Data Analysis

To effectively manage data collection the researcher proactively incorporated qualitative coding, (Appendix B). The researcher used descriptive, topic, and analytical qualitative coding procedures (Richards, 2010). Further, the researcher used qualitative

61

analysis software, Nvivo9 to identify categories, patterns, and relationships of the data (Richards, 2010). This provided the researcher with an additional unbiased, objective research tool to ensure accuracy and reliability of the data.

Validity and Reliability

A focus group research approach with the qualitative methodology provides the researcher with the opportunity and challenge to conduct effective, meaningful, and detail rich information specific to proposed research/interview questions. Narrowing down the scope to specific interview questions that are tailored to address the proposed research questions allows for tailored approach to obtaining specific data that addresses the research questions (Berlin & Snow, 2009; Creswell & Miller, 1997; Greenbaum, 2000; Huberman, 2002; Miles & Huberman, 1994; Seale, Gobo, Gubrium, & Silverman, 2004) The interactions and data provided built validity and reliability to the specific research questions. The participants of the study have relevant, applicable, and direct experience dealing with integration preparation of organizational culture, human capital management, and change management for mergers and acquisitions. Having this direct experience provides practitioner- focused data about the research questions; which ultimately provides objective sense of validity and reliability to the data collection (Creswell, 2003; Creswell & Miller, 2000; Eisenhardt, 2006; Krueger & Casey, 2000; Malterud, 2001; Morgan & Smiricich, 1980).

Furthermore, the setting and format of interaction was conducted in a safe, comfortable, and easy to access environment which allowed the participants to engage and participate with the interview questions either verbally and/or non-verbally, through directly messaging the researcher during the focus group interview. Also, the direct, secure, and instant digital recording of the focus group interviews provided an unbiased, objective recording of the interviews. To add to the objective nature of a frequently referred to subjective methodology, the use of a secure, reliable, unbiased, and objective transcription software, Dragon directly incorporated the verbal audio recording into Microsoft Word. Electronic transcription documents were processed with a computer aided qualitative software program that organized, grouped, and served as an additional tool for analysis. All of which illustrate a proactive approach to ensure the objectivity of the data collection and data analysis throughout the process to yield a greater reliability and credibility of the research study.

Ethical Considerations

The first and most important objective of the research study is ensuring the safety, well-being, understanding, and benefits of participation for the participants (Capella University, 2010; Creswell, 2003; Creswell & Miller, 1997; Greenbaum, 2000; Huberman, 2002; Seale, Gobo, Gubrium, & Silverman, 2004). Participants were fully informed about the purpose of the study, participation within the study, the risks, the benefits and value of contributing to the study (Appendix D). Furthermore, respect for participants' identities, schedules, communication preferences, and interview interactions were given.

Security of the participant information and data collection is of the utmost importance, data, including: digital audio recordings of the focus group interviews, electronic transcriptions, qualitative computer aided data analysis, and analysis materials does not contain personal identifiers of the participants. Further, the information was stored in a password protected internal and external hard-drive accessible to the

63

researcher, data will viewed and discussed between the researcher, mentor, and committee members who have all received ethical training certification. The data will be stored for at least five years on the researcher's primary computer.

CHAPTER 4. RESULTS

Introduction

The purpose of this research study was twofold, to identify how HRM practitioners incorporate organizational culture, human capital management, and change management into an integration preparation plan for mergers and acquisitions. Secondly, whether or not having an integration plan influenced the integration process. The research questions of these areas provided the start to the data investigation. The research findings are organized consistently to the interview questions:

1. Was there an HR -oriented integration preparation plan completed – yes or no?

2. What integration preparation was done for organizational culture, human capital management, and change management? Were these areas done separately or simultaneously?

3. How did the integration preparation or the lack thereof influence the integration of the acquired or merged companies?

The following areas of this section will address those questions, responses, and analysis of those responses.

Qualitative Research Queries Conducted as Part of Data Analysis

Nvivo 9, qualitative research software was used to organize and identify interview responses. The researcher removed all identifiers and replaced with corresponding participant number, uploaded the summary pre-screening questionnaire table, and interview transcriptions to Nvivo 9. The researcher created appropriate descriptive, topical, and analytical qualitative coding schemes consistent as shown in Appendix B, Qualitative Coding Scheme. Appendix C, Participant Descriptive provides a breakdown of non-identifier information about participants that correspond to the descriptive coding categories listed in Appendix B. Qualitative Coding Schemes. Participant Transcripts were used to identify specific coding themes. Appendix D. Coding Summary Reports of Questions to Responses provides a breakdown of themes per responses

It is essential to clarify that Nvivo 9 does not analyze the data, but serves as a tool for the researcher to organize, identify, and locate themes within the data. Data analysis was done by the researcher based on review of these materials. Data results, themes, and analysis follow incrementally through interview responses in the following sections.

Participants

Table 2 Participant Descriptive and Table 2 Participant Descriptive Quantified provides a visual breakdown of this section. Initially, there were eighteen prospective participants; however, only fourteen were interviewed. This yielded a response rate of 72%. However, it is essential to point out that five of the prospective participants were not qualified to participant and one was a no show participant. Thirteen participants met the sample size requirements and were interviewed. Twelve of those participants were top-level HRM executives employed within publically traded and privately held organizations. One participant was a middle-level HRM employed with a publically traded organization. Eight participants have a Master's degree. Four participants have a Bachelor's degree. One participant has a doctoral degree. Two participants have SPHR Certification. One participant has PHR and GPHR certification.

Five participants experienced integration preparation in a merger and acquisition in 2011. Four participants experienced integration preparation in a merger and acquisition 2010 and 2008. One participant experienced a merger and acquisition in 2009. Thirteen

66

participants described the merger and acquisition as "friendly" and one participant

describe the merger and acquisition as "hostile".

Table 2. – Participant Attributes

Participant	HRM Career Level	Education	HR Certifications	M&A Year	Friendly or Hostile	Public or Private
P1	Top	Master's	SPHR	2008	Friendly	Private
P2	Top	Master's	SPHR	2010	Friendly	Private
P3	Middle	Bachelor's	PHR, GPHR	2008	Friendly	Public
P4	Top	Master's	None	2010	Friendly	Private
P5	Top	Bachelor's	None	2010	Hostile	Public
P6	Top	Bachelor's	None	2010	Friendly	Private
P7	Middle	Master's	None	2008	Friendly	Public
P8	Top	Master's	International	2011	Friendly	Private
P9	Top	Master's	None	2008	Friendly	Private
P10	Top	Master's	None	2011	Friendly	Public
P11	Top	Bachelor's	None	2011	Friendly	Public
P12	Top	Master's	None	2011	Friendly	Public
P13	Top	Doctorate	None	2011	Friendly	Public

Table 3. Participant Attributes Quantified

HRM Career Level	Quantity	Education	Quantity	HR Certifications	Quantity	M&A Year	Quantity	Friendly or Hostile	Quantity	Public or Private	Quantity
Top	11	Bachelor's	4	SPHR	2	2008	4	Friendly	12	Public	7
Middle	2	Master's	8	PHR	1	2009	0	Hostile	1	Private	6
		Doctorate	1	GPHR	1	2010	4				
				International	1	2011	5				
				None	7						

Question 1: HR Oriented Integration Preparation Completed?

The purpose of this question was to identify whether or not HR related integration

preparation was completed. All participants reported yes, however, participant three

noted a yes and no response. Participant 3 noted that there was integration preparation completed at the executive levels, however, communication to mid-level HR practitioners was poor.

Overall, all participants noted that there was HR oriented integration preparation. However, for data analysis purposes of this first interview question, participants noted that integration preparation does occur. The interview question however is closed-ended, with a yes or no response, so there is significant depth and detail not included in the responses. That depth and detail surfaces in the experiences to the integration preparation for organizational culture, human capital management, and change management are discussed in the following sections.

Question 2 (a): Integration Preparation for Organizational Culture?

This section presents the data collected regarding organizational culture integration preparation. Data within this section presented three overlapping themes: comprehensive, limited, and no organizational culture integration preparation. Additional qualitative detail is discussed in the following paragraphs.

Table 4. Question 2(a) Organizational Culture (OC) Integration Preparation

Participant	OC Comprehensive	OC Limited	OC None	HRM Career Level	Education	HR Certifications	M&A Year	Friendly or Hostile	Public or Private
P1		1		Top	Master's	SPHR	2008	Friendly	Private
P2	1			Middle	Bachelor's	PHR, GPHR	2008	Friendly	Public
P3			1	Middle	Master's	None	2008	Friendly	Public
P4	1			Top	Master's	None	2008	Friendly	Private
P5		1		Top	Master's	SPHR	2010	Friendly	Private
P6		1		Top	Master's	None	2010	Friendly	Private
P7	1			Top	Bachelor's	None	2010	Hostile	Public
P8	1			Top	Bachelor's	None	2010	Friendly	Private
P9	1			Top	Master's	International	2011	Friendly	Private
P10		1		Top	Master's	None	2011	Friendly	Public
P11	1			Top	Bachelor's	None	2011	Friendly	Public
P12	1			Top	Master's	None	2011	Friendly	Public
P13		1		Top	Doctorate	None	2011	Friendly	Public
Quantity	7	5	1						

Table 4 provides a brief visual representation of theme categories; however, additional data analysis is required. 92% of respondents noted that there was integration preparation done for organizational culture. However, from those respondents, the level of planning varied from generic to comprehensive. In fact, 46% of respondents discussed that organizational culture was limited, and 46% was extensive, and eight percent did no organizational culture integration preparation. By limited, the most commonly referenced was that they knew culture was important, but when it came right down to effectively researching it, there was no consistent plan in place to identify, measure, or analyze culture. Rather, analysis of culture happened as a result of underlying assumptions that surfaced from external research, discussions, and meetings. These underlying assumptions led to misunderstandings about the actual organizational cultures. In hindsight, this is one of the respondents would have liked to know more about the comprehensive resources used to measure organizational culture. By comprehensive, these respondents created, implemented, measured, and analyzed comprehensive findings about organizational culture to customize their organizational culture integration strategy.

Within this study, there was a split between respondents of limited and comprehensive integration preparation for organizational culture. Limited respondents noted initially with their responses that there was integration planning for organizational culture, however, that the planning was subpar. Subpar, within the context of the responses to this interview question, means that the respondents reported their experiences with organizational culture preparation as not fully effective, generic, and limited in functionality. At face value, the data indicated integration preparation was completed for organizational culture, however, through deeper analysis of responses the

69

level of preparation varied significantly. The differences will be discussed in more depth in the following paragraphs of this section, including best practices noted for organizational culture integration preparation.

Analysis: Organizational Culture Integration Preparation

This section is the analysis of themes within the limited, comprehensive, and no organizational culture integration preparation approaches.

Data Analysis: Limited Organizational Culture Integration Preparation

To begin, it is helpful to point out the themes of the limited organizational culture integration category. The themes include: external research about the organizations, making assumptions of culture based on interactions with executives in meetings, focusing only on the culture of the headquarters or one primary location and not on subcultures of different business units, and lastly, a limited understanding of approaches to investigate organizational culture. The following four paragraphs will analyze the four aforementioned themes.

External research about the organizational cultures of the organizations involved in the merger and acquisition at face level sounds reasonable. is that it provided This provided participants with reasonable access to information quickly, affordably, and the flexibility of not having to leave their own organizations. This is similar research strategies for most individuals. Is this strategy flawed? There may not be a definitive answer to that question, but is the strategy limited? Again, this depends on the perspective of what would constitute limited. Yes, it is limited in depth and detail about the actual organizational cultures. The internet, discussion forums, or databases provide a relevant, credible, and quick approach to gaining information. However, the accuracy of that information may vary and not appropriately reflect the actual organizational culture. Furthermore, it does not address subcultures found in departments, business units, or other geographic locations.

The purpose of conducting organizational culture research is to get a better understanding of the current culture. Online research through the corporate websites, discussion forums, and databases may provide some external insight, but as shown through respondents' experiences is very limited to effectiveness of integration preparation. It may be useful to note that corporate communications, such as corporate websites are written by public relations. This could cause a integration bias based on the perception of organization culture as it is seen by public relations. Ultimately, this approach to analysis of organization is limited to because it may not be an accurate representation of the actual organizational culture. The limited nature this type of external research, may be a factor in the next approach used within the limited organizational culture integration category, which included assumptions based on interactions with executives in meetings. Founders, executives, and management certainly impact organizational culture based on integrating their values, beliefs, and standards within their organizations. However, limiting the analysis of culture based on interactions with executives during meetings is biased to the perspectives of the executives. These interactions, as described by respondents were more discussions about the deals, not about culture per se. More about their visions about what value the organizations bring to the deal, not the underlying shared beliefs, values, and standards that represent the identity of organizational culture.

71

Organizational culture is based on *shared* experiences, values, and beliefs about internal standards and operational activities. No organization is staffed only with executives; they have employees of different levels, specialties, and so on within their organization. To limit organizational culture perspectives to only that of observation of interactions between executives or to limited external research undermines organizational culture altogether. The people within the organization, including executives, are what set the tone and standards of physical and non-physical attributes of organizational culture. Keeping in mind that executives certainly orchestrate operational activities, executives are not alone in carrying out strategy. Strategy is carried out by employees, and understanding the organizational culture as it reflects an organization, should also reflect employees' perspective of organizational culture.

Lastly, the limited research of headquarters' corporate culture according to the executive posed a limitation to organizational culture integration preparation. Respondents noted that although, headquarters' organizational culture was important and played a role in integration preparation, however, it did not address the problem of not investigating subcultures. This was the case in multi-location organizations that had multiple business units. Corporate cultures may have looked on the surface to be complimentary, however, after the fact integration; subunit cultures that were not included in the organizational culture preparation caused setbacks in the buy in of implementing post-merger activities.

In conclusion, limited organizational culture integration preparation respondents shared the following themes: organizational culture biased by executive leadership perspectives, headquarter organizational culture analysis, limited external research about

72

organizational culture, assumptions about culture based on interactions from meetings, and lack of analysis of subcultures. Respondents noted that although the research and analysis may have been limited it did provide information about organizational culture that was used in organizational culture integration preparation. However, the effectiveness of the information was limited, as noted through areas that appeared during integration that were not identified in the initial organizational culture due diligence nor implemented in integration preparation.

Data Analysis: Comprehensive Organizational Culture Integration Preparation

This section will focus on the data analysis of respondents that noted comprehensive organizational culture integration preparation. To do this, the analysis will include identification and analysis of the areas that corresponded with participants' perspectives of comprehensive organizational culture integration preparation. Those areas included: significant time for preparation, research, and analysis of exploring organizational culture prior to integration preparation.

The time spent on analyzing organizational culture varied from one to six months. In terms, of time, how long respondents had to investigate influenced the approach used. Participants noted the length of time prior to announcement of a merger and acquisition influenced the level of detail, analysis, and planning that was done to investigate organizational culture. There was a split response in the specific amount of time that information was provided to management about the likelihood of moving forward with a deal. Several of the respondents noted this was because of the legal ramifications of actions prior to announcing the deal. This again, varied from publically traded and private organizations. However, even within both types of organizations, respondents noted the

73

importance of time for the effectiveness of the organizational culture due diligence. The timeframes noted from participants, including public and private organization, ranged from one to six months.

It is relevant to note here, that all participants in this category are top-level HRM professionals. Participants shared their level of understanding about the time constraints, organizations, and approaches helped to create a plan to evaluate organizational cultures. This plan, as noted by participants was only discussed with other executive management. No internal or external communication was completed about any intention of merging or acquiring an organization. This was because at this stage of due diligence not much is said before any announcement, this known as the quite phase. Like investigating whether or not there will be a fit between partners, there needs to be time to conduct that research. The time to conduct that research effectively, review and analysis it accordingly was paramount in moving forward or not with the deal.

What was consistent is that all participants that noted comprehensive organizational culture that had one to six months for organizational culture integration preparation noted that it was enough time to conduct the organizational culture due diligence. Participants noted timeframe differences from one to six months to conduct organizational culture due diligence and put together appropriate organizational culture integration approaches. Participants that organized merger and acquisition teams appeared to have less initial upfront time invested in conducting organizational culture due diligence and preparation. This was because of the internal strategy of identification of roles, responsibilities, and timeframes of this type of due diligence. Furthermore, participants that noted this type of internal capabilities were from organizations that

74

routinely incorporate mergers or acquisitions as part of their growth strategies. In these cases, participants noted time playing a key role in not only the effectiveness of research, but also the effectiveness of moving forward sooner to achieve appropriate organizational culture integration objectives. Moreover, participants noted the sooner organizational cultures were aligned, the sooner there could be buy in from employees, and buy in promotes behavior to carry out organizational objectives.

Participants noted that time had a significant impact on the level of research and analysis of organizational culture due diligence and integration preparation. Consistent with time was the level of attention and use to appropriate tools to identify, measure, and analyze organizational culture. Participants noted the following techniques: on-site visits to observe environments, interactions, and processes; customized organizational culture surveys and face-to -face interviews with executives at headquarters. One or more of these techniques were used simultaneously or separately by participants.

On-site visits to observe organizational culture environments appeared to be use less than other techniques. However, participants that used this approach noted the importance of objectivity provided an in-depth richness of detail which surveys appeared to omit. The richness of data came from immersing oneself into the environment of another organization. Noting the similarities and differences between the organizational cultures was essential to the culture analysis. However, subjectivity of analysis could also limit the perception of the actual organizational culture. Furthermore, whether or not this analysis was done by a team or just one person could be helpful the credibility of the objective culture.

In addition, as noted the subjective energy about the prospective deal could also influence the objective analysis in an on-site organizational culture analysis. Meaning, that if the prospective merger or acquisition has been noted by executive management as an "excellent" opportunity and the transfer of the perception of "excellent" could impair the analysis of the actual organizational culture. This could also limit providing specific concerns about the culture because of managements' concern about moving forward and not addressing concerns that could undermine that from occurring. Furthermore, HRM professionals are the ones that carried out these organizational cultures on-site audits. Leaving room for prospective bias to the previous subjectivity concern linked with executive management perspective of the deal.

The use of external HRM organizational culture consultants was noted by participants to conduct on-site audits as beneficial. This was because the external consultants were contracted to carry out an unbiased analysis of the organizational cultures and report the findings accordingly. This took the approach of comparing both organizational cultures separately by a contracted third party consultant. This was just strictly a due diligence action to provide an external appraisal of organizational cultures. If applicable, the analysis would then be used internally to create an appropriate integration plan.

Besides conducting on-site organizational culture audits, participants noted the use of customized organizational culture surveys. These surveys were created by internal HRM professionals or were already incorporated as the organization's approach to identifying culture by the integration team. These surveys ranged in the quantity of questions. However, the themes of questions were consistent in the following areas:

leadership styles, power, innovation, and change. These surveys were provided to executive management for completion, return, and analysis.

Customized organizational culture surveys provided HRM professionals will relatively specific information about organizational culture quickly, securely, and were relatively direct to review. This helped speed up the analysis process of organizational culture according to the responses. However, the gap of the analysis lies in the only executive management was surveyed. Executive management certainly influences, shapes, and should be able to relatively pinpoint organizational culture, however, organizational culture is shared standards, attitudes, beliefs and values of all employees within the organization. Certainly, a sample of only executive management does not reflect the entire organizational culture.

Furthermore, the customized organizational culture surveys were provided to executive management, depending on the confidentiality of the responses, executives may not fully disclose the organizational culture. The reasons for limited disclosure could range from: anonymity, not wanting to bring up troublesome culture traits, not seeing culture as important, or just wanting to move forward with the deal and hastily completing the survey to get to the next step. Respondents noted that the data with the customized surveys may provide specific detail to main areas of concern, but may not entirely reflect all areas about organizational culture. For example, participants from serial acquirers noted special areas concerning power and innovation being their main culture concerns. Other organizational culture areas were secondary, but based on past experiences with acquisitions; power and innovation were the core areas that were pivotal to moving forward or not.

The last core area of comprehensive organizational integration preparation respondents was the influence analysis of organizational culture data. All respondents within this question noted that the analysis of organizational culture tailored the strategy of organizational culture integration preparation. Common themes of analysis included: maximizing similarities, minimizing differences, and respecting corporate and subunit organizational cultures.

Focus on core complementary cultures was used within integration preparation. This was to link together similarities that the organizational cultures and create a sense of connection prior to actual integration. This sense of connection would provide increase awareness of acceptance of particular aspects of organizational culture. This was consistent with the concept of the flywheel principle because focus was on the positive culture traits. This built integration preparation organizational culture momentum that maximized attitudes towards integration. By maximizing similar core values in organizational culture the integration of those areas were more easily accepted and adopted. This also helped to minimize resistance in other organizational culture areas because of strategizing attentions to the similarities.

The respondents indicated that differences in organizational culture were not ignored; however, deeper analysis of those differences had to happen. The analysis of differences provided HRM professionals and integration team professionals with data about core areas that could potential hamper the acceptance, development, and maintenance of an integrated organization. However, a couple of participants noted that the organizational cultures were so extreme that the best strategy for survival was to keep the organizational cultures separate. Best practices to handling differences was

78

communication, respect, and adapting; even if adapting means not integrating the organizational cultures. Furthermore, there was consistency that neglecting to address differences head on during the due diligence integration preparation stage was careless. Nonetheless, blatantly ignoring differences to focus on similarities happens and unfortunately undermines some areas of effectiveness.

In conclusion, comprehensive organizational culture integration preparation respondents shared the following themes: time, research, and analysis. However, within those areas there were subthemes that impacted the effectiveness organizational culture integration preparation. The most noteworthy areas of concerns included: executive leadership bias, subjectivity of objective organizational culture audits, organizational culture survey participants, including only executive leadership and focus of headquarter organizational culture. Best practices to those challenges included: external organizational culture audits, analysis of external culture reports, incorporating management at different levels, and creating an environment that respects and hears all concerns about organizational culture.

Data Analysis: No Organizational Culture Integration Preparation

One respondent noted that there was no organizational culture integration preparation completed. This was because the main areas of integration preparation were human capital management, contracts, and ensuring legal compliance before, during, and after the merger. The respondent noted that organizational culture due diligence would have probably helped with the integration, however, because of the focus of core areas according to executive leadership, organizational culture was not considered to be a driving influence to the integration of the merger.

79

Conclusion: Organizational Culture Integration Preparation

Respondents from limited, comprehensive, and none categories provided in-depth detail about their organizational culture integration preparation experiences. Limited and comprehensive categories shared similar concerns that could undermine the effectiveness of organizational culture integration preparation: saturated executive leadership, subjectivity biases, and disregard to subcultures or business unit cultures, and lastly, environments which were not fully open to hearing discrepancies, and planning for those differences. Best practices noted by participants: integration preparation team customized organizational culture techniques, detailed analysis, use of third-party organizational culture consultants, and lastly maintaining respect for organizational cultures throughout the integration preparation process. Furthermore, full or partial integration intentions were considered to be paramount to determining appropriate integration preparation.

Question 2 (b): Integration Preparation for Human Capital Management

This section is the analysis of themes within the comprehensive and limited human capital management integration preparation approaches. Table 5 2(b) Human Capital Management (HCM) Integration Preparation provides a visual summary representation of responses and participant attributes. However, additional analysis of each of these areas will be discussed in the following paragraphs.

Table 5. 2(b) Human Capital Management (HCM) Integration Preparation

Participant	HCM Comprehensive	HCM Limited	HCM None	HRM Career Level	Education	HR Certifications	M&A Year	Friendly or Hostile	Public or Private
P1	1			Top	Master's	SPHR	2008	Friendly	Private
P2		1		Middle	Bachelor's	PHR, GPHR	2008	Friendly	Public
P3		1		Middle	Master's	None	2008	Friendly	Public
P4	1			Top	Master's	None	2008	Friendly	Private
P5	1			Top	Master's	SPHR	2010	Friendly	Private
P6	1			Top	Master's	None	2010	Friendly	Private
P7	1			Top	Bachelor's	None	2010	Hostile	Public
P8	1			Top	Bachelor's	None	2010	Friendly	Private
P9	1			Top	Master's	International	2011	Friendly	Private
P10		1		Top	Master's	None	2011	Friendly	Public
P11	1			Top	Bachelor's	None	2011	Friendly	Public
P12	1			Top	Master's	None	2011	Friendly	Public
P13		1		Top	Doctorate	None	2011	Friendly	Public
Quantity	9	4	0						

Data Analysis: Comprehensive Human Capital Management Integration Preparation

All but one participant noted that identification, analysis, and creation of human capital management integration preparation were comprehensive. This section is the analysis of the human capital management themes: executive human capital analysis, workforce planning, HR processes and infrastructure, compensation, benefits, payroll, and legal. The level of identification, analysis, and implementation of the aforementioned human capital management themes varied per participant; however, there was significant overlap.

All participants within this category noted that there was extensive executive human capital analysis completed. This included identification and analysis of executive management. This included: research and analysis about executive leadership roles, responsibilities, qualifications, limitations, compensation, succession planning, and severance packages. To do this, the following techniques were noted: internal research, structured interviews with executives, and one-to-one mark approach to placement of executives within the integrated organization.

Internal research included documentation about executives' roles, responsibilities, length of employment, performance analytics, qualifications, and compensation. This information served to provide a greater scope into the executive leadership within the organization. Furthermore, it served as quantitative and qualitative data used to take inventory of the executives. This inventory was then scrutinized by internal executives, top-level HRM executives, and/or external human capital management consultants.

Identification of strengths and limitations of executives was taken into account and appropriate decisions were made regarding continuing or severing employment. A participant noted that the one-to-one mark approach was used to retain or terminate employment. The one-to-one mark approach focused on fairness of placement of equal executives within the new integrated organization. This approach was not focused on the qualifications of executives or the best suited executive for the position. A straight-line method about compensation and responsibilities was also used to reduce redundancies in costs and labor. This approach was noted as more quantifiable and less concerned with the human factor of talent.

In addition to human capital analysis in terms of cost benefits -analysis and executive inventory, workforce planning analysis was also identified as an area of comprehensive analysis for integration preparation. For example, a participant noted the need to increase the current combined workforce of five hundred employees to seven hundred employees over the next twelve months. This required effective workforce planning to determine the job functions, skills, recruitment, and placement aspects. This also required analysis of both pre-merger human capital and post-merger human capital needs. The analysis required understanding of the specific internal differences for the positions, changes after the merger, and ensuring consistency of new recruitment and training of prospective employees.

Internal HR processes and infrastructure was also analyzed. This included evaluating HR processes, policies, and systems. HR processes and infrastructure is the administrative and technological core of the HR department that organizes, evaluates, and maintains all HR related information. This information includes: compensation, benefits, payroll, policies, legal, and performance evaluations. Participants noted that significant time was spent understanding these internal HR functions because of the core to HR activities. Participants also noted that activities such as mind-share (knowledge management), discussions, and on-site visits were used to collaborate the similarities, differences, and create a best practice integration of the internal HR processes and infrastructure.

Compensation analysis played a more crucial role in that of executives compared to non-management to middle-management positions. However, depending participants noted that a comparable compensation analysis of similar positions. This was especially the case when combining employees within one organization. The reasoning behind this analysis and implementation to human capital management integration preparation was to promote a fairness principle. What changes that happened with compensation were communicated through multiple mediums: face to face, email, letters, and town hall meetings.

Benefits were also analyzed. This information was identified through the organizations during due diligence. This information was reviewed, discussed, and depending on the type of merger or acquisition, the HRM executives selected the "best fit" benefits package for the new organization. However, as noted, depending on the type of merger or acquisition the level of analysis varied. Participants noted that if the deal was an acquisition to buy up the competition, with no real intent to continue operations afterwards there was limited review of the benefits. Furthermore, whether integration was going to be partial or full also impacted the level of analysis and benefits integration preparation. Comparable, participants that noted a traditional full integration of organizations combining under one new organization analysis and benefits integration preparation was completed the yielded the greatest fairness.

Most participants noted that payroll was also researched, analyzed, and an appropriate integration preparation plan was implemented. Participants noted the payroll issues as a concern. Ensuring consistency and timeliness with the delivery of compensation was noted as paramount to employees. Ironically, participants noted that this was essential to prevent concern of integration as a result of payroll delays or issues. These issues are technically areas that most executives do not think about, but if neglected impact employee morale. Employee morale influences the productivity of integration objectives. Overcoming the pay check battle helps to build trust and respect with employees which is necessary with obtaining integration objectives.

Research, analysis, and appropriate strategy were incorporated regarding legal aspects of human capital management. These legal aspects included: contracts, litigation, and legislation. Contracts ranged from employment, intellectual, and union contracts.

84

Depending on the size and scope of the merger and acquisition, the level of analysis of one or more of these contractual areas varied. For instance, some participants noted significant time with the legal analysis and preparation of union contracts, shared services, and intellectual property. Whereas, other participants were concerned with current litigation and employment contracts in the organizations. Current HR legal issues were investigated comprehensively and appropriate integration preparation to ensure consistent legal protocol was performed.

In conclusion, the aforementioned areas were considered comprehensive human capital management areas of research, analysis, and incorporated within integration preparation. It is relevant to note that the majority of respondents noted that all of these areas were rolled out independently by prospective subject matter experts of those areas. Those experts include internal and/or external consultants. This was because of the timing, resources, and subject knowledge requirements. The analysis and creation of appropriate human capital management integration was discussed by top-level HRM professionals and implemented accordingly. In most cases, there was a checklist or integration team of subject matter experts in these areas to make the most effective use of resources and time to complete the human capital management integration preparation.

Data Analysis: Limited Human Capital Management Integration Preparation

Limited human capital management preparation within the perception of participants means that integration preparation was subpar compared to what was done after the announcement of the deal. So, for purposes of this data analysis it is essential to understand that the level of research, analysis, and preparation of human capital management areas were considered to be limited in the overall effectiveness of

85

integrating the human capital management areas. The remainder of this section will identify, discuss, and analyze the common limited human capital management themes: recruitment processes and one-to-one mark approach used to place executive management.

Integration preparation for recruitment processes was noted as limited by one participant. This was because the analysis, planning, and communication of recruitment process integration to mid-level HRM were subpar. By subpar, there was no internal communications or coaching about the recruitment process to mid-level HRM until after the changes happened. Furthermore, when integration did occur, mid-level HRM was sent unannounced to the acquired organization and told to implement the recruitment processes. There was no support or direction in terms of how to change the recruitment process, other than to make it more consistent to the acquirer's process. The acquired HRM staff did not even realize they were acquired. This caused tension, frustration, and inefficiencies with recruitment process integration. Furthermore, two years later, the recruitment processes have not fully integrated and are performing in subpar manner.

The use of the one-to-one mark approach to selecting and placing executive management was noted as limited approach. The one-to-one mark approach is based on the fairness principle of placing an equal amount of executive talent into new roles of the new organization. Participant noted that this approach undermined qualifications for fairness. The idea is that fairness would create a greater unity; however, it caused frustration because of placing less qualified executives into positions that required specific qualifications. These frustrations influenced executives' attitudes, which in turned caused turnover, and impacted the overall effectiveness of carrying out executives' objectives.

Conclusion: Human Capital Management Integration Preparation

In conclusion, recruitment processes and one-to-one mark approaches were identified as limited within human capital management integration. This was a result of planning within these areas. Specifically, participants noted neglecting research and implementation of approaches consistent with integration fit. Rather, one participant noted the approach selected was about fairness, not practicality. Another participant noted the disregard to any integration planning prior to the integration. In both cases, the limited integration preparation of caused tension, frustration, and turnover.

Question 2 (c): Integration Preparation for Change Management?

This section is the analysis of themes within the comprehensive and limited change management integration preparation. Table 6 2(c) Change Management (CM) Integration Preparation provides a visual summary representation of responses and participant attributes. However, additional analysis of each of these areas will be discussed in the following paragraphs.

Table 6. 2(c) Change Management (CM) Integration Preparation

Participant	CM Comprehensive	CM Limited	CM None	HRM Career Level	Education	HR Certifications	M&A Year	Friendly or Hostile	Public or Private
P1		1		Top	Master's	SPHR	2008	Friendly	Private
P2	1			Middle	Bachelor's	PHR, GPHR	2008	Friendly	Public
P3			1	Middle	Master's	None	2008	Friendly	Public
P4	1			Top	Master's	None	2008	Friendly	Private
P5		1		Top	Master's	SPHR	2010	Friendly	Private
P6	1			Top	Master's	None	2010	Friendly	Private
P7	1			Top	Bachelor's	None	2010	Hostile	Public
P8	1			Top	Bachelor's	None	2010	Friendly	Private
P9		1		Top	Master's	International	2011	Friendly	Private
P10		1		Top	Master's	None	2011	Friendly	Public
P11	1			Top	Bachelor's	None	2011	Friendly	Public
P12	1			Top	Master's	None	2011	Friendly	Public
P13		1		Top	Doctorate	None	2011	Friendly	Public
Quantity	7	5	1						

Data Analysis: Comprehensive Change Management Integration Preparation.

Comprehensive change management integration preparation consisted of the following themes: understanding the actual changes, communication, buy-in, and tracking. Participants noted that change management appeared to be a direct part integration preparation of organizational culture and human capital management, and not necessarily a standalone area within integration preparation. Yet, also noted was that specific changes in all integration preparation areas were had implementation plans. However, the aforementioned themes provided comprehensive perspective of change management integration preparation. Therefore, the remainder of this section will discuss understanding the actual changes, communication, buy-in, and tracking change management themes.

Before change can occur, participants noted the importance of understanding what those changes were , why they were happening, how the changes would come about, and how the changes would impact employees. A clear understanding of these changes helps with the integration of the actions needed to make these changes occur. This

88

understanding should happen throughout the due diligence and analysis stages prior to integration. So, that the integration preparation is effective of addressing the changes that will happen at integration. For many participants, this was the reason why change management happened at the time during organizational culture and human capital management integration preparation.

Effective communication of changes is essential to changes actually be heard, received, anticipated, and implemented. Participants noted communication should be clear, honest, and direct. This is to minimize confusion and tension to change. Furthermore, as noted by participants multiple mediums should be used to confirm and reaffirm communications, such as: emails, letters, town hall meetings, webinars, intranet communication releases, and face–to- face communication with management. Participants also noted that communication planning should also anticipate the perception of how communication may be viewed by employees. Communication planning is done by top-level HRM. This in turn, may not fully reflect perceptions of employees. However, as best-practice, as noted by participants is to plan a communication strategy around the receiving audience.

Buy-in was noted as paramount to change management. According to participants, buy- in requires purpose, motivation, and direction. This means creating a united understanding regarding why changes are happening, how changes will impact employees personally and professionally, how these changes will be better than the current system, and the actions required to move change in the required directions. Creating a unity between the current and prospective systems is important, but the reason, motivation, and actions needed to get to the prospective system promote a greater acceptance of changes. The greater understanding, the greater probability of acceptance, and the greater likelihood of actions required to make changes happen.

Tracking change management was also incorporated with change management integration preparation. This was done more heavily with integration preparation teams. The tracking mechanism served to provide a plan to monitor specific changes within organizational culture and human capital management. Phases, milestones, or objective dates were created based on management analysis. Tracking encompassed the use of project management tools, HRIS interfaces, and management communications. Integration team professionals would update the integration preparation database regularly.

In conclusion, comprehensive change management integration preparation was noted by participants as an indirect action of organizational culture and human capital management integration preparation. Change within organizational culture and human capital management would require active management. Participants that used integration preparation teams also incorporated change management integration preparation. Whether change management occurred separately or simultaneously participants shared the following themes: understanding change, communication, buy-in, and tracking change. However, the level of incorporation and preparation of change management varied. Participants noted a consistent gap with the message of change. Specifically, tailoring the what, why, and how message about change to fit with the employees' perspective. Participants noted the positive influence of employees' prospective perspective of change prior to the announcement of change. This helped to customize a more receptive message about the change. However, all communications were based on top-level management perspective of employees' perceptions of change. Which often was noted was not an accurate reflection and impacted the receptiveness of change.

Data Analysis: Limited Change Management Integration Preparation.

One participant noted limited change management integration preparation was completed. The participant was a middle-level HRM that noted no preparation to handle change was completed for organizational culture or human capital management. The participant noted top-level HRM may have done some form of change management planning, however, the limited communication about organizational culture, human capital management, or that an acquisition happened was not shared with mid-level management. The participant noted had there been effective participation in those areas that would have minimized the conflict, tension, and perhaps, not left so many integration errors two years after the integration.

In conclusion, the overarching theme within the limited change management was change management should have incorporated all of the changes within organizational culture and human capital management. However, because there was subpar communication of any and all changes in those areas to mid-level management there did not appear effective integration preparation in any of those areas. The lack of integration preparation and/or communication flawed the entire integration preparation.

Conclusion: Change Management Integration Preparation

Comprehensive change management integration preparation was noted by participants as an indirect action of changes within organizational culture and human capital management integration preparation. Whether change management occurred separately or simultaneously participants shared the following themes: understanding

91

change, communication, buy-in, and tracking change. However, the themes required understanding the perspective of change recipients, yet no interaction with change recipients were noted by participants. Furthermore, no interaction and lack of communication from top-level to middle-level HRM was noted as a fundamental limitation of change management integration.

Question 2 (d): Were Organizational Culture, Human Capital Management, and Change Management Integration Preparation Completed Separately or Simultaneously?

Six participants noted separately. Six noted simultaneously. One participant noted that integration preparation of those areas occurred both separately and simultaneously. Participants that noted simultaneously also incorporated an integration preparation model. Table 7. Question 2(d) Simultaneous or Separate Integration Preparation provides a visual representation of data in this section.

Table 7. 2(d) Simultaneous or Separate Integration Preparation

Participant	Simultaneous	Separate	Both	HRM Career Level	Education	HR Certifications	M&A Year	Friendly or Hostile	Public or Private
P1		1		Top	Master's	SPHR	2008	Friendly	Private
P2	1			Middle	Bachelor's	PHR, GPHR	2008	Friendly	Public
P3		1		Middle	Master's	None	2008	Friendly	Public
P4	1			Top	Master's	None	2008	Friendly	Private
P5	1			Top	Master's	SPHR	2010	Friendly	Private
P6		1		Top	Master's	None	2010	Friendly	Private
P7			1	Top	Bachelor's	None	2010	Hostile	Public
P8		1		Top	Bachelor's	None	2010	Friendly	Private
P9	1			Top	Master's	International	2011	Friendly	Private
P10	1			Top	Master's	None	2011	Friendly	Public
P11		1		Top	Bachelor's	None	2011	Friendly	Public
P12	1			Top	Master's	None	2011	Friendly	Public
P13		1		Top	Doctorate	None	2011	Friendly	Public
Quantity	6	6	1						

CHAPTER 5. DISCUSSION, IMPLICATIONS, RECOMMENDATIONS

Research Problem

The problem of this study is the disconnection of research of integration preparation for HRM practitioners of organizational culture, human capital management, and change management. The perspective of the problem within this study is to focus in on integration preparation of these areas that have shown to individually influence integration value creation and a conceptual connection of these areas. Connecting the disjointedness of these areas will add to and create value to the field of integration preparation of these areas for HRM practitioners. Specifically, this study may potentially impact the effectiveness of integration preparation for HRM practitioners. The potential for HRM practitioners to have a connected conceptual framework for integration preparation may provide greater integration of these areas.

Relevance and Types of Literature Reviewed

Current and peer-reviewed literature was reviewed regarding: integration, organizational culture, human capital management, change management, and mergers and acquisitions. This research was relevant to scope of this study because it provided depth and perspective about core areas of this research study. Furthermore, the literature review also revealed the research problem: the disjointedness of the research areas within integration preparation for HRM practitioners.

Methodology

The researcher used a phenomenological approach. This approach allowed the researcher to gain qualitative data based on the experiences of participants about a particular phenomenon. Merger and acquisition integration failure to achieve proposed objectives is the phenomenon in this study. This is because up to 65% of mergers and acquisitions fail and the frequently cited reason for failure is the poor integration of organizational culture, human capital management, and change management. These areas often fall under scope of HRM. Therefore, a phenomenological methodology provided the researcher with data based on HRM practitioners' integration preparation experiences.

The researcher conducted online focus group interviews and independent online interviews. The purpose of the online focus group interviews was to provide a medium of interaction to stimulate this discussion of the interview questions between participants. The concept was that with two or more participants greater detail would surface. However, participants' responses and experiences did not change between focus group interviews and independent interviews. The independent interviews were a result of scheduling differences between participants, no-shows, or a participant's request not to share experiences with other participants. The collaboration of experiences provided meaningful, relevant, and direct responses to the research questions.

Discussion of Study's Findings

This section will briefly discuss the main themes of the data collected about organizational culture, human capital management, and change management integration preparation. This section is organized according to interview question themes. These themes were consistent with the literature review findings of these areas, however, also sparked challenges and best practices.

Question 1: HR Oriented Integration Preparation Completed

All participants responded yes. This was also pre-screening requirement for participants to ensure that participants had actually experienced integration preparation. The experience is necessary to the overall methodology that studies the experiences of a particular phenomenon, which in this case is integration preparation. Therefore, there was a consensus shared with participants that integration preparation was completed and they had participated in some form of the integration preparation.

Question 2 (a): Integration Preparation for Organizational Culture?

All participants noted that organizational culture integration preparation was essential. However, the level of integration preparation for organizational culture varied. For instance, 46% of participants considered the organizational culture integration preparation completed was comprehensive. On the other hand, 46% also considered organizational culture integration preparation limited. Eight percent did not complete any form of organizational culture integration preparation. These findings indicated a relatively similar split between comprehensive and limited organizational culture integration preparation. Furthermore, it also indicated that while organizational culture is perceived to be essential, more than half of the participants did limited or no organizational culture integration preparation. Ultimately, the limited or no organizational culture integration preparation impacted the overall effectiveness of organizational culture integration.

The biggest challenges that impacted the limitedness of organizational culture integration preparation included: non-adequate timeframes for preparation, external research about the organizations, making assumptions of culture based on interactions

95

with executives in meetings, focusing only on the culture of the headquarters or one primary location and not on subcultures of different business units, and lastly, a limited understanding of approaches to investigate organizational culture. These areas each bring up internal issues with organizational culture integration preparation. The researcher's analyses of those challenges are located in the Conclusions section.

Although, participants' experiences illustrated limitedness within organizational culture integration preparation, best practices surfaced from experiences of participants that noted comprehensive preparation. Best practices included: external organizational culture audits, analysis of external culture reports, incorporating management at different levels, and creating an environment that respected and heard all concerns about organizational culture. However, even within the best practices, the following concerns carrying out the best practices surfaced throughout the discussions: executive leadership bias, subjectivity of objective organizational culture audits, organizational culture surveyed only executive leadership, and focus was again primarily on headquarters' organizational culture.

One participant noted that no organizational culture integration preparation was completed because it was not perceived to be a primary concern for executive management. This was because the primary concerns were within human capital management, including, but not limited to: contracts, legal compliance, and other compensation. The participant also noted that organizational culture investigation would have probably helped with the integration, but that it was not a primary concern and therefore, there was no prior integration preparation for organizational culture.

96

Question 2 (b): Integration Preparation for Human Capital Management

All but one participant noted that identification, analysis, and creation of human capital management integration preparation were comprehensive. The human capital management integration focus areas included: executive human capital analysis, workforce planning, HR processes and infrastructure, compensation, benefits, payroll, and legal. Best practices within these areas included: an integration preparation team that delegated the areas to subject matter experts, streamlined analysis of human capital management, and effective communication to bring about appropriate changes to human capital management areas.

One participant noted human capital management integration preparation was limited because of the lack of coordination, communication, and implementation of changes from executive management to middle management. Integration preparation was completed within the traditional human capital management areas; however, it was done by executive management and not properly transferred to mid-level management that carried out the human capital management integration objectives.

Question 2 (c): Integration Preparation for Change Management

Overall, participants noted that comprehensive change management was indirectly and directly implemented within integration preparation. The biggest difference in responses was whether change management was completed as its own separate part of integration preparation or if it was indirectly a part of the organizational culture and human capital management integration changes. Participants noted the level of preparation for change was similar to comprehensiveness and limited natures presented within organizational culture and human capital management integration preparation

97

areas. This question also brought up a greater response for the use of integration preparation teams that managed the areas of change. However, whether change management was done by an integration preparation team or independent HRM professionals the following themes regarding change were shared: understanding change, communication, buy-in, and tracking change.

One participant that noted limited change management integration preparation explained it as a result of subpar communication and coordination integration preparation within organizational culture and human capital management. The limited integration preparation within those areas transferred to limited change management of those areas. The participant noted the lack of integration preparation and/or communication flawed the entire integration preparation

Question 2 (d) Were Organizational Culture, Human Capital Management, and Change Management Integration Preparation Completed Separately or Simultaneously?

Equal participants noted separately or simultaneously. While, one participant noted integration preparation of those areas occurred both separately and simultaneously. Meaning, separate integration preparation was completed for organizational culture, human capital management, and change management, however, the integration preparation happened at the same time. This was a result of working on multiple separate areas within the overall integration preparation.

Implications

This section discusses the implications for organizational culture, human capital management, and change management integration preparation. Furthermore, additional research analysis of what these themes may indicate in light of the study's initial research questions:

1. How do HRM practitioners incorporate organizational culture, human capital management, and change management into an integration preparation plan for a merger and acquisition?

2. How does having an integration preparation plan influence integration of organizational culture, human capital management, and change management throughout the process?

This section will provide readers with practical and theoretical insight of the ramifications of this study, as well as the limitations. This will be done in order of the initial research questions.

Implications - Research Question 1: How do HRM Practitioners Incorporate Organizational Culture, Human Capital Management, and Change Management into an Integration Preparation Plan for a Merger and Acquisition?

Participants noted three approaches to incorporating organizational culture, human capital management, and change management into an integration preparation plan:

1. Internal integration team – to simultaneously address organizational culture, human capital management, and change management integration preparation, or

2. External integration team – same functions as above, however, external HRM subject matter experts were hired, or

3. Separate internal HR professionals investigate and create the organizational culture, human capital management, and change management integration preparation plan.

The aforementioned approaches to indicate that organizational culture, human capital management, and change management are incorporated within an integration preparation plan. However, each approach varies organizationally based on the specific integration needs within those areas.

Internal Integration Preparation Team Approach

An internal integration preparation team was frequently cited by participants as the preferred approach to deal with integration. The purpose of this approach was to identify the core integration areas, establish due diligence research strategies, create milestones, and delegate integration responsibilities. Basically, this approach served to address all of the HR integration preparation needs completed by one integration team. The team approach was used to break down the complexity and depth of organizational culture, human capital management, and change management integration needs. Furthermore, team members were selected to complete integration research, analysis, and implementation of integration preparation based on expertise. For example, organizational culture specialists were delegated to the organizational culture function of the integration preparation team. This was to promote effectiveness based on placing the most qualified specialists in those roles. However, not every organization had enough internal specialists which caused some employees to be put in integration roles with inadequate level of knowledge about that particular integration area.

External Integration Team Approach

The purpose of this approach was to select the most qualified HRM external consultants to provide customized, unbiased, and extensive research, analysis, and creation of organizational culture, human capital management, and change management integration preparation. Using this approach allowed internal HRM professionals to continue with normal HR operations. External consultants helped to streamline integration preparation and provided customized integration consulting services. Participants that used this approached noted comprehensive and effective organizational culture, human capital management, and change management integration preparation.

Separate Internal HR Professionals Investigate and Create Integration Preparation Plan

This approach used internal executive HRM professionals to research, analyze, and create the organizational culture, human capital management, and change management integration preparation plan. These areas were then handled independently and separately from other integration areas. Participants noted challenges with this approach: communication, resources, and not being able to fully identify all areas that should have been implemented within the integration preparation plan. The effectiveness of this approach varied between comprehensive and limited organizational culture, human capital management, and change management.

Implications Research Question 1 – Conclusion

In conclusion, the aforementioned approaches to integration preparation have been used by participants. Whatever approach used requires customization, analysis, and implementation of best practices. Furthermore, it is essential to be aware of challenges.

101

Such as ineffective matching of internal resources or setting too complex expectations on internal or external integration teams. The objective of integration preparation is to provide an effective approach to integration, to promote sustainability and longevity of effectiveness in a merger or acquisition, and profitability. Subpar preparation within integration preparation research, talent, resources, time, or communication could impair effectiveness. Therefore, adequate attention to internal and external capabilities, resources, and methodologies for integration preparation is paramount to the effectiveness of all three approaches.

Implications - Research Question 2: How does having an Integration Preparation Plan Influence Integration of Organizational Culture, Human Capital Management, and Change Management throughout the Process?

This section will discuss the implications of having an integration preparation plan influences on integration of organizational culture, human capital management, and change management throughout the integration process. To do this, implications of each section will be discussed separately. Lastly, an overall conclusion of the implications will be discussed.

Integration Preparation Plan Influence on Organizational Culture Integration

Organizational culture integration preparation was identified by participants as essential. However, seven participants perceived comprehensive integration preparation. Six had limited to no integration preparation. The perception that organizational culture integration preparation was essential, however, the actual level and effectiveness of organizational culture preparation varied.

In theory, organizational culture integration is essential to participants, however, actual effectiveness varied between participants. Five participants noted limited integration preparation as a result of subpar resources, time, communication, one-dimensional analysis of headquarters' culture, and executive biases. From those five participants three were from private organizations and two from publically traded organizations. The sole participant that noted no organizational culture integration preparation was completed was from a publically traded organization. This was noted because organizational culture was not seen as a primary integration concern. Likewise, four of the seven participants noted comprehensive integration preparations were from publically traded organizations. That being said the responses between limited, none, and comprehensive are relatively consistent. So, the results would imply that yes, organizational culture is known as essential to integration, however, the depth and effectiveness of organizational culture integration preparation was almost equivalent between comprehensive and limited.

Integration Preparation Plan Influence on Human Capital Management Integration

Since nine out of thirteen participants noted comprehensive human capital management integration preparation was completed implies a greater priority over organizational culture integration preparation. However, six of the nine participants were from privately held organizations. Interesting to note, all four participants that noted limited were from publically traded organizations. Although there was an increase in comprehensive integration within human capital management compared to organizational culture that was more dramatically seen within participants from privately owned organizations.

Participants from publically traded organizations noted that the level of integration preparation prior to the announcement of the merger or acquisition was a determining factor on integration preparation. However, integration preparation does not have to just occur only before the actual announcement. This yields concern about the level of human capital management integration preparation. Furthermore, human capital management integration plans can be created to effectively identify, analyze, and implement appropriate human capital management integration actions.

Integration Preparation Plan Influence on Change Management Integration

Participants noted integration preparation change management was not necessarily an independent section of integration preparation. This implies that there is not always a standalone change management integration preparation section. Participants noted that change management occurred within organizational culture and human capital management did not require a section specific to change management. However, seven participants noted comprehensive, five noted limited, and one noted no change management integration preparation.

Five of the seven participants noted comprehensive change management were from publically traded organizations. This is interesting given that this was contrary to human capital management integration of publically traded organizations. This does not make sense because how can there be more comprehensive change management than human capital management when whatever changes that would be managed would have to deal with human capital management or organizational culture. Perhaps, this was the result of confusion with the term of change management.

104

Equally interesting is that only two participants from privately held organizations noted comprehensive change management integration preparation. There was significantly more comprehensive human capital management integration preparation within privately held organizations, yet significantly less change management integration preparation occurred. This could imply that overall change management integration preparation was conducted compared to specific areas within organizational culture or human capital management.

Implications Research Question 2 – Conclusion

Overall, eleven participants noted organizational culture, human capital management, and change management integration preparation was effective to the overall integration process. Two participants noted ineffective. Those two participants were from publically traded organizations. However, there appears to be significant emphasis on organizational culture as essential to integration preparation, but almost half of the participants noted limited or no organizational culture integration preparation. This implies an inconsistency between theory and what is being done practically. Furthermore, there is a significance difference between comprehensive and limited human capital management integration preparation between publically-traded and privately-owned organizations.

Limitations

The focus group interview approach provided the researcher with the opportunity to gain additional insight into participants' experiences; however, some participants were reluctant or nervous to share those experiences with other participants. Accommodating participants that preferred independent interviews to share their experiences to the interview questions could limit the findings. However, the interview questions were the same for all participants. Furthermore, all participants answered the interview questions according to their personal experiences. So the core phenomenological methodology was still achieved through the analysis of those experiences about the phenomenon of this research study. Lastly, the sample size does not necessarily reflect the responses or actions of integration preparation.

Conclusion

The purpose of this study was to create an integration preparation framework for HRM practitioners. The purpose spurred from the disconnected research about integration preparation. The disconnectedness occurred in organizational culture, human capital management, and change management integration preparation practices. Each area has shown to be crucial within integration. The research problem and questions were answered, however, additional research would benefit to the body of HRM integration preparation knowledge. Overall, HRM integration preparation was identified as essential to integration effectiveness. However, similar to the disconnectedness of research, there were differences between integration preparation experiences. These differences may be a result of the level of preparation and understandings of theoretical and practical integration preparation approaches. Therefore, the researcher was able to identify recommendations within an integration preparation framework, however, identified disconnectedness between research and professional integration preparation practices.

Recommendations Developed Directly from Data

This research study presented a number of comprehensive and some limited experiences to organizational culture, human capital management, and change

106

management integration preparation. From these experiences, successful and challenging themes surfaced. The following integration preparation best practices should be considered by practitioners going through integration preparation:

- HRM practitioners should establish a balance participation of different levels of management within integration preparation. An unbalanced integration preparation team could cause biases, take away value, and not accurately reflect core areas within integration preparation. This balance also includes having the right talent involved in the integration preparation to ensure best fits, skills, and expertise to carry out integration preparation roles and responsibilities.

- Evaluate measurements organizational culture prior to implementing the approaches to the integration preparation. Identify the best fit organizational culture measure methodology that is both cost and time effective. HRM practitioners should not forget to measure organizational cultures of subunits and different geographic areas. Do not rely on assumptions from discussions with executive or meetings to paint a "full and accurate" picture of the overall organizational culture. Organizational culture is the result of shared experiences that set the standards, norms, values, and beliefs within an organization. Organizational culture exists throughout all kinds of organizations.

- HRM practitioners should identify, analyze, and implement a human capital management integration preparation plan that is customized to the specific merger or acquisition. This may vary in private and public organizations. Additional research about acceptable integration preparation prior to announcement should be investigated and communicated appropriately within the integration team.

107

Whatever the case may be, human capital management integration preparation was noted as one of the core areas to integration preparation, but was the least effective with integration preparation.

- HRM practitioners should identify the best approach to change management within integration preparation. This can include a standalone change management integration preparation section or simultaneously incorporate changes within organizational culture or human capital management integration preparation sections. Whichever approach, the changes should be easily identified, measurable, and monitored.

- HRM practitioners need to establish and facilitate communication best practices for integration preparation. Communication of changes across the board in all integration preparation areas is essential. Communication transfer from levels of management, organizations, business units, geographic regions, and different forms of communication. Best practices noted from this study included: putting yourself in the shoes of communication receivers, open and honest, form of communications (town hall meetings, group meetings, emails, corporate announcements, and independent communications), and lastly, balance frequency of communication. The more specific and meaningful the communication integration preparations plan the more effective the overall integration preparation and actual integration.

Although the aforementioned best practices may not cover all integration preparation best practices, based on this research study these overarching themes directly influenced the overall integration preparation effectiveness.

Recommendations for Further Research

This research study investigated HRM experiences to integration preparation. Challenges and best practices of those experiences provide the aforementioned recommendations directly from the data, however, the study also promoted additional areas for future research. The areas for future research may provide HRM practitioners with additional insights about integration preparation that are specific to the type of merger or acquisition. This may include:

- Research effectiveness integration preparation teams of only executives, mixed levels of management, hybrid teams that have internal and external integration specialists, and no integration preparation team.

- Research the effectiveness of external HRM consultants. It would be interesting to study the best practices of internal and external HRM consultants to see if there are overarching differences in communication, speed, value, timeframe, and overall effectiveness.

- Research the start time and areas of focus of integration preparation by internal integration preparation teams and external consultants. This would be interesting to identify timeframes of due diligence, incorporation of research in integration preparation, and differences between these areas in publically-traded and privately owned organizations.

- Research regarding internal HRM integration preparation communication practices. The following communication challenges should be investigated: limited communication transfer, lack of clarity of integration changes, and creating an environment that welcomes open communication among integration preparation professionals.

- Research organizational culture integration preparation differences, including: measurements, approaches, and effectiveness. Noting approaches in multi-locations and different business units.

- A study of friendly versus hostile HRM integration preparation experiences.

- Research experiences of the HRM professionals of mergers and acquisitions that were previous to 2008.This could include follow-up research of practitioners that experienced friendly and hostile mergers and acquisitions. Including analysis of acquirer and acquired experiences.

REFERENCES

Adams, B., & Woo, K., (2011). US M&A news and trends. *FactSet*. Retrieved from: http://www.factset.com/websitefiles/PDFs/general/flashwiremonthly1_11/ .

Allred, B. B., Boal, K. B., & Holstein, W. K. (2005). Corporations as stepfamilies: A new metaphor for explaining the fate of merged and acquired companies. *Academy of Management Executive, 19*(3), 23-37.

Almor, T., Tarba, S. Y., & Benjamini, H. (2009). Unmasking integration challenges: The case of biogal's acquisition by teva pharmaceutical industries. *International Studies of Management & Organization, 39*(3), 32-52. doi:10.2753/IMO0020-8825390302

Alvesson, M., & Karreman, D., (2007). Unraveling HRM: identity, ceremony, and control in management consulting firm. *Organization Science,* 18(4), 711-723.

Amabile, T., Patterson, C., Mueller, J., Wojcik, T., Odomirok,J., Marsh, T., & Kramer, S., (2001). Academic-practitioner collaboration in management research: A case of cross-profession collaboration. *Academy of Management Journal,* 44(2), 418-431. Retrieved February 17, 2011, from ABI/INFORM Global. (Document ID: 71974781).

Argyris, C. (1997). Initiating change that perseveres. *American Behavioral Scientist, 40*(3), 299.

Badrtalei, J., & Bates, D. L. (2007). Effect of organizational cultures on mergers and acquisitions: The case of Daimler Chrysler. *International Journal of Management, 24*(2), 303-317.

Barki, H. & Pinsonneault, A., (2005). A model of organizational integration, implementation effort, and performance. *Organization Science,* 16(2), 165-179.

Barkema, H.G., & Schijven, M., (2008). Toward unlocking the full potential of acquisitions: The role of organizational restructuring. *Academy of Management Journal, 51*(4), 696-722.

Beard, M. J., & Zuniga, L. C. (2006). Achieving the right flavor: A study of designing a cultural integration process. *Psychologist-Manager Journal, 9*(1), 13-25. doi:10.1207/s15503461tpmj0901_3

Berg, B.L. (2004). *Qualitative research methods for social sciences.* Boston: Pearson.

Berlin, G., & Solow, R. (2009). Get the question right, then choose the method. *Journal of Policy Analysis & Management, 28*(1), 175-176. doi:10.1002/pam.20414

Bligh, M. C. (2001). From culture clash to integration: The role of leadership in transforming post-merger employee identification. (Ph.D., State University of New York at Buffalo). , 179.

Bradbury-Jones, C., Irvine, F., & Sambrook, S., (2009). The phenomenological focus group: an oxymoron? *Journal of Advanced Nursing, 65*(3), 663-671.

Budhwar, P. S., Varma, A., Katou, A. A., & Narayan, D. (2009). The role of HR in cross-border mergers and acquisitions: The case of indian pharmaceutical firms. *Multinational Business Review, 17*(2), 89-110.

Buono, A. F. (2005). Mergers and acquisitions: Managing culture and human resources. *Administrative Science Quarterly, 50*(4), 647-650.

Burnes, B., (2004). Kurt Lewin and the planned approach to change: a reappraisal. *Journal of Management Studies.* 41(6), 977-1002.

Caldwell, R., (2006). Champions, adapters, consultants, and synergists: the new change agents of HRM. *Human Resource Management Journal,* 11(3), 39-52.

Cartwright, S., Cooper, C. L., Cartwright, S., & Cooper, C. L. (1993). Organizational culture measure. *Human Relations, 46,* 327-347.

Cartwright, S., & Schoenberg, R. (2006). Thirty years of mergers and acquisitions research: Recent advances and future opportunities. *British Journal of Management, 17,* S1-S5. doi:10.1111/j.1467-8551.2006.00475.x

Chakrabarti, R., Gupta-Mukherjee, S., & Jayaraman, N., (2009). Mars-Venus marriages: culture and cross-border M&A. *Journal of International Business Studies,* 40, 216-236.

Chanmugam, R., Shill, W., Mann, D., Ficery, K., & Pursche, B., (2005). The intelligent clean room: ensuring value capture in mergers and acquisitions. *Journal of Business Strategy,* 25(3), 43-49.

Chatman, J. A., & Eunyoung Cha, S. (2003). Leading by leveraging culture. *California Management Review, 45*(4), 20-34.

Chatterjee, S., Lubatkin, M., Sweiger, D., & Weber, Y., (1992). Cultural differences and shareholder value in related mergers: linking equity and human capital. *Strategic Management Journal,* 13, 319-334.

Clark, S. M., Gioia, D. A., Ketchen, J.,David J., & Thomas, J. B. (2010). Transitional identity as a facilitator of organizational identity change during a merger. *Administrative Science Quarterly, 55*(3), 397-438.

Collins, J.C., (2010). Good to great: why some companies make the leap – and others don't. New York, NY: Harper Business.

Cording, M., Christmann, P., & King., D. (2008). Reducing causal ambiguity in acquisition integration: Intermediate goals as mediators of integration decisions and acquisition performance. *Academy of Management Journal, 51*(4), 744-767.

Creswell, J. W. (2003). Research Design Qualitative Quantitative and Mixed Methods Approaches (2nd ed.). Thousand Oaks, CA: Sage Publishing Inc.

Creswell, J. W., & Miller, D. L. (2000). Determining validity in qualitative inquiry. *Theory into Practice, 39*(3), 124.

Creswell, J. W., & Miller, G. A. (1997). Research methodologies and the doctoral process. *New Directions for Higher Education,* (99), 33.

Datta, D. K. (1991). Organizational fit and acquisition performance: Effects of post-acquisition integration. *Strategic Management Journal, 12*(4), 281-297.

Datta, D. K., Pinches, G. E., & Narayanan, V. K. (1992). Factors influencing wealth creation from mergers and acquisitions: A meta-analysis. *Strategic Management Journal, 13*(1), 67-84.

de Camara, D., & Renjen, P., (2005). The secrets of successful mergers: dispatches from the front lines. *Journal of Business Strategy*, 25(3), 10-14.

de Haldevang, B. (2009). A new direction in M&A integration: How companies find solutions to value destruction in people-based activity. *Global Business & Organizational Excellence, 28*(4), 6-28. doi:10.1002/joe.20264

DePamphillis, D., (2007). *Mergers, Acquisitions, and Other Restructuring Activities* (4th ed.). Burlington, MA: Academic Press.

Devinney, T., Midgley, D., & Venaik, S., (2000). The optimal performance of the global firm: formalizing and extending integration – responsiveness framework. *Organization Science*, 11 (6), 674-695.

DiGeorgio, R. M. (2002). Making mergers and acquisitions work: What we know and don't know -- part I. *Journal of Change Management, 3*(2), 134.

DiGeorgio, R. M. (2003). Making mergers and acquisitions work: What we know and don't know--part II. *Journal of Change Management, 3*(3), 259.

Dumon, M., (2008). Biggest merger and acquisition disasters. Investodpedia, ULC.

Eisenhardt, K. M. (1991). Better stories and better constructs: The case for rigor and comparative logic. *Academy of Management Review, 16*(3), 620-627.

Eisenhart, M. (2006). Qualitative science in experimental time. *International Journal of Qualitative Studies in Education (QSE), 19*(6), 697-707. doi:10.1080/09518390600975826

Eriksson, M., & Sundgren, M. (2005). Managing change: Strategy or serendipity— reflections from the merger of Astra and Zeneca. *Journal of Change Management, 5*(1), 15-28. doi:10.1080/14697010500036007

Fairbairn, U. (2005). HR as a strategic partner: Culture change as an American Express case study. *Human Resource Management, 44*(1), 79-84. doi:10.1002/hrm.20043

Fawcett, S. E., Brau, J. C., Rhoads, G. K., Whitlark, D., & Fawcett, A. M. (2008). Spirituality and organizational culture: Cultivating the ABCs of an inspiring workplace. *International Journal of Public Administration, 31*(4), 420-438. doi:10.1080/01900690701590819

Fish, D. (2007). A study of entropy in post-merger and post-acquisition integration. (D.B.A., University of Phoenix). , 396.

Froese, F., Pak, Y., & Chong, L., (2008). Managing the human side of cross-border acquisitions in South Korea. *Journal of World Business*, 43 (2008), 97-108.

Greenbaum, T. (2000). Moderating focus groups: a practical guide for group facilitation. Thousand Oaks, CA: Sage.

Haleblian, J., Devers, C. E., McNamara, G., Carpenter, M. A., & Davison, R. B. (2009). Taking stock of what we know about mergers and acquisitions: A review and research agenda. *Journal of Management, 35*(3), 469-502.

Hendry, C., Pringle, J., & McLafferty, E., (2011). Phenomenological approaches: challenges and choices. *Nurse Researcher*, 18(2), 7-18.

Higgins, J. M., & McAllaster, C. (2004). If you want strategic change, don't forget to change your cultural artifacts. *Journal of Change Management, 4*(1), 63-73. doi:10.1080/1469701032000154926

Hofstede, G., Neuijen, B., Ohayv, D. D., Sanders, G., Arnold, T., & Spell, C. S. (2006). Organizational culture measure. *Journal of Business and Psychology, 20*(4), 599-620.

Homburg, C., & Bucerius, M. (2006). Is speed of integration really a success factor of mergers and acquisitions? An analysis of the role of internal and external relatedness. *Strategic Management Journal, 27*(4), 347-367.

Hubmerman, M., & Miles, M. (2002). The qualitative research companion. Thousand Oaks, CA: Sage.

Jick, T. D. (1979). Mixing qualitative and quantitative methods: Triangulation in action. *Administrative Science Quarterly, 24*(4), 602-611.

Keener, C. (2009). Choreographing distressed integration. *Mergers & Acquisitions: The Dealermaker's Journal, 44*(7), 40-54.

Kendra, K., & Taplin, L. J. (2004). Project success: A cultural framework. *Project Management Journal, 35*(1), 30-45.

Kephart, J. (2010). Common experiences of courage among executives associated with merger cultural integration. (Ed.D., Pepperdine University). , 188.

Kiessling, T., & Harvey, M. (2005). Strategic global human resource management research in the twenty-first century: An endorsement of the mixed-method research methodology. *International Journal of Human Resource Management, 16*(1), 22-45. doi:10.1080/0958519042000295939

Knodel, T. (2004). Preparing the organizational 'soil' for measurable and sustainable change: Business value management and project governance. *Journal of Change Management, 4*(1), 45-62. doi:10.1080/1469701032000154935

Kotter, J., (1996). Leading change. *Harvard Business Press:* Boston, MA.

Kotter, J., (2002). *The heart of change: real-life stories how people change their organizations.* Harvard Business Press: Boston, MA.

Kotter, J., (2008). A sense of urgency. *Harvard Business Press:* Boston, MA.

Krueger, R., & Casey, M.A. (2000). *Focus groups: a practical guide for applied research.* Thousand Oaks, CA: Sage.

Larsson, R., & Finkelstein, S., (1999). Integrating strategic, organizational, and human resource perspectives on mergers and acquisitions: a case survey of synergy realization. *Organization Science,* 10(1), 1-26.

Larsson, R., & Lubatkin, M., (2001). Achieving acculturation in mergers and acquisitions: an international case survey. *Human Relations,* 54(12), 1573-1607.

Lawler, E. E. III, & Mohrman, S. A. (2000). Beyond the vision: What makes HR effective? *Human Resource Planning, 23*(4), 10-20.

Lawler, E. E. III, & Mohrman, S. A. (2003). HR as a strategic partner: What does it take to make it happen? *Human Resource Planning, 26*(3), 15-29.

Levin, I., & Gottlieb, J. Z. (2009). Realigning organization culture for optimal performance: Six principles & eight practices. *Organization Development Journal, 27*(4), 31-46.

Lewin, K., (1947). Chapter five: quasi-stationary social equilibria and the problem of permanent change. *Organization Change.*

MacDonald, J. (2010). Value creation in pharmaceutical mergers. (Ph.D., Capella University). , 105.

Malterud, K., (2001). Qualitative research: standards, challenges, and guidelines. *The Lancelet, 35*(358), 483-488.

Marks, M.L. & Mirvis, P.H., (2010). Joining forces: making one plus one equal three in mergers, acquisitions, and alliances. San Francisco, CA: Jossey-Bass.

Marks, M. L., & Vansteenkiste, R. (2008). Preparing for organizational death: Proactive HR engagement in an organizational transition. *Human Resource Management, 47*(4), 809-827.

Martin, T. N., & Huq, Z. (2007). Realigning top management's strategic change actions for ERP implementation: How specializing on just cultural and environmental contextual factors could improve success. *Journal of Change Management, 7*(2), 121-142. doi:10.1080/14697010701531749

McNamara, G. M., Haleblain, J., & Dykes, B. J. (2008). The performance implications of participating in an acquisition wave: Early mover advantages, bandwagon effects, and the moderating influence of industry characteristics and acquirer tactics. *Academy of Management Journal, 51*(1), 113-130.

Mitleton-Kelly, E. (2006). Coevolutionary integration: The co-creation of a new organizational form following a merger and acquisition. *Emergence: Complexity & Organization, 8*(2), 36-47.

Mohrman, S. A. (2007). Designing organizations for growth: The human resource contribution. *Human Resource Planning, 30*(4), 34-45.

Morgan, G., & Smircich, L. (1980). The case for qualitative research, *Academy of Management Review*, 491-500.

Moustakas, C. E., (1994). *Phenomenological research methods*. Thousand Oaks, CA: *Sage.*

Münner, M. G. (2007). Personal transformation as a leverage for organizational transformation. the TEA program as a facilitator of cultural change management. *Organization Development Journal, 25*(4), P49-P54.

Nadler, D. A. (1982). Managing transitions to uncertain future states. *Organizational Dynamics, 11*(1), 37-45.

Nadler, D. A., & Tushman, M. L. (1989). Organizational frame bending: Principles for managing reorientation. *Academy of Management Executive (08963789), 3*(3), 194-204.

Nadler, D. A., & Tushman, M. L. (1999). The organization of the future: Strategic imperatives and core competencies for the 21st century. *Organizational Dynamics, 28*(1), 45-60.

Neghab, A. E. P., Sardari, N., & Imani, S. (2009). A model to evaluate organization capability for business process reengineering with respect to organizational culture. *International Journal of Business Research, 9*(2), 87-93.

Paine, F. T., & Power, D. J. (1984). Merger strategy: An examination of Drucker's five rules for successful acquisitions. *Strategic Management Journal, 5*(2), 99-110.

Polyhart, R., Weekley, J., & Baughman, K. (2006). The structure and function of human capital emergence: a multi-level examination of the attraction-selection-attrition model. *Academy of Management Journal*, 49(4) 661-677.

Puranam, P., Singh, H., & Chaudhuri, S. (2009). Integrating acquired capabilities: When structural integration is (un)necessary. *Organization Science, 20*(2), 313-328.

Ravasi, D., & Schultz, M., (2006). Responding to organizational identity threats: exploring the role of organizational culture. *Academy of Management Journal,* 49(3), 433-458.

Rees, C., & Edwards, T. (2009). Management strategy and HR in international mergers: Choice, constraint and pragmatism. *Human Resource Management Journal, 19*(1), 24-39. doi:10.1111/j.1748-8583.2008.00087.x

Riad, S. (2005). The power of 'organizational culture' as a discursive formation in merger integration. *Organization Studies (01708406), 26*(10), 1529-1554. doi:10.1177/0170840605057072

Richards, L., (2010). *Handling qualitative data – a practical guide*. Thousands Oaks, CA: Sage.

Schiemann, W. A. (2006). People equity: A new paradigm for measuring and managing human capital. *Human Resource Planning, 29*(1), 34-44.

Schein, E. H. (1983). The role of the founder in creating organizational culture. *Organizational Dynamics, 12*(1), 13-28.

Schein, E. H. (1990). Organizational culture. *American Psychologist, 45*(2), 109-119. doi:10.1037/0003-066X.45.2.109

Schein, E. H. (1996). Culture: The missing concept in organization studies. *Administrative Science Quarterly, 41*(2), 229-240.

Schein, E. H. (1997). Organizational culture and leadership (2nd ed.). San Francisco, CA: Jossey-Bass.

Schein, E. H. (1999). Kurt Lewin's change theory in the field and in the classroom: Notes toward a model of managed learning. *Reflections, 1*(1), 59-74. doi:10.1162/152417399570287

Schein, E. H. (2002). Models and tools for stability and change in human systems. *Reflections, 4*(2), 34-46. doi:10.1162/152417302762251327

Schein, E. H. (2003). Five traps for consulting psychologists: Or, how I learned to take culture seriously. *Consulting Psychology Journal: Practice and Research, 55*(2), 75-83. doi:10.1037/1061-4087.55.2.75

Schein, E. H., Goffee, R., & Jones, G. (1997). What holds the modern company together? *Harvard Business Review, 75*(6), 174-176.

Schmidt, J., (2008). *Making mergers work – the strategic importance of people*. Alexandria, VA: SHRM Foundation.

Seale, C., Gobo, G., Gubrium, J., & Silverman, D. (2004). Qualitative research practice. Thousand Oaks, CA: Sage.

Shaver, J. M. (2006). A paradox of synergy: Contagion and capacity effects in mergers and acquisitions. *Academy of Management Review, 31*(4), 962-976.

Smollan, R., & Sayers, J. (2009). Organizational culture, change and emotions: A qualitative study. *Journal of Change Management, 9*(4), 435-457. doi:10.1080/14697010903360632

Sorenson, O., Mcevily, S., Ren, C. R., & Roy, R. (2006). Niche width revisited: Organizational scope, behavior and performance. *Strategic Management Journal, 27*(10), 915-936.

Stahl, G., & Voigt, A. (2008). Do cultural differences matter in mergers and acquisitions? A tentative model and examination. *Organization Science, 19*(1), 160-176.

Swaminathan, V., Murshed, F., & Hulland, J. (2008). Value creation following merger and acquisition announcements: The role of strategic emphasis alignment. *Journal of Marketing Research (JMR), 45*(1), 33-47. doi:10.1509/jmkr.45.1.33

Valant, L. B. (2008). Why do both marriages and business mergers have a 50% failure rate? *CPA Journal, 78*(8), 15-15.

Van Dijk, R., & Van Dick, R. (2009). Navigating organizational change: Change leaders, employee resistance and work-based identities. *Journal of Change Management, 9*(2), 143-163. doi:10.1080/14697010902879087

Vosburgh, R. M. (2007). The evolution of HR: Developing HR as an internal consulting organization. *Human Resource Planning, 30*(3), 11-23.

Wan, Y. (2008). Managing post-merger integration: A case study of a merger in Chinese higher education. (Ph.D., University of Michigan). , 252.

Wickramasinghe, V., & Karunaratne, C., (2009). People management in mergers and acquisitions in Sri Lanka: employee perceptions. *The International Journal of Human Resource Management,* 20(3), 694-715.

Yin, R. K. (1984). Beyond method: Strategies for social research. *Administrative Science Quarterly, 29*(2), 321-323.

Zollo, M., & Meier, D. (2008). What is M&A performance? *Academy of Management Perspectives, 22*(3), 55-77.

Zollo, M., & Singh, H. (2004). Deliberate learning in corporate acquisitions: post-acquisition strategies and integration capability in U.S. bank mergers. *Strategic Management Journal,* 25, 1233-1256.

APPENDIX A. PARTICIPANT PRE-SCREENING QUESTIONNAIRE

Question	*Response*
Are you an HRM practitioner with three or more years of HRM experience?	**Yes or No**
What was your position title at the time of the M&A?	**Title:**
What is your highest level of education completed?	**HS ; Associates ; Bachelors; Masters; Doctorate**
Do you have any HR certifications? If so, which one(s)?	**Yes or No** **If yes, type of certification (s):**
Was the M&A within last five years?	**Yes or No**
Was it a friendly or hostile M&A?	**F or H**
Did you participate during the integration process?	**Yes or No**

APPENDIX B. QUALITATIVE CODING SCHEMES

Descriptive Coding Categories	Topical Coding Categories	Analytical Coding Categories
HRM Position/Title Years in the position	Integration Preparation (IP) for Organizational Culture	Q2(a) – Comprehensive, Limited or None IP Organizational Culture
Years in HRM	IP for Human Capital Management	Q2(b) Comprehensive, Limited, or None IP Human Capital Management
Year of M & A	IP for Change Management	Q2 (c) Comprehensive, Limited, or None IP Change Management
	Integration Preparation	Q3(a, 1) Separately, Simultaneously, or Both.
Education Level	Perceived Effectiveness of Integration Preparation Performance on M&A	Q3 (a, 2) IP Effective or IP Ineffective
HRM Certification Type of M&A		

APPENDIX C. PARTICIPANT DESCRIPTIVES

Participant	HRM Career Level	Education	HR Certifications	M&A Year	Friendly or Hostile	Public or Private
P1	Top	Master's	SPHR	2008	Friendly	Private
P2	Top	Master's	SPHR	2010	Friendly	Private
P3	Middle	Bachelor's	PHR, GPHR	2008	Friendly	Public
P4	Top	Master's	None	2010	Friendly	Private
P5	Top	Bachelor's	None	2010	Hostile	Public
P6	Top	Bachelor's	None	2010	Friendly	Private
P7	Middle	Master's	None	2008	Friendly	Public
P8	Top	Master's	International	2011	Friendly	Private
P9	Top	Master's	None	2008	Friendly	Private
P10	Top	Master's	None	2011	Friendly	Public
P11	Top	Bachelor's	None	2011	Friendly	Public
P12	Top	Master's	None	2011	Friendly	Public
P13	Top	Doctorate	None	2011	Friendly	Public

APPENDIX D. CODING SUMMARY REPORTS

Coding Summary

Integration Planning - Dissertation

12/4/2011 1:11 PM

Hierarchical Name	Aggregate	Coverage	Number Of Coding	Number Of Users Coding
Dataset				
Internals\\Pre-Screening Questionnaire Survey - Descriptive				
Node				
Nodes\\Archive\\GPHR	No	3.17%	1	1
Nodes\\Archive\\International Certification	No	7.14%	1	1
Nodes\\Archive\\PHR	No	2.38%	1	1
Document				
Internals\\Participant 1				
Node				
Nodes\\Archive\\Participant 1	No	100.00%	1	1
Nodes\\HR Integration Preparation Completed	No	0.14%	1	1
Nodes\\Questions - Topical Coding Categories\\Question 1	No	2.58%	1	1
Nodes\\Themes\\Change Management Integration Planning\Change Management - None	No	10.30%	1	1
Nodes\\Themes\\Communication	Yes	4.69%	0	1
Nodes\\Themes\\Communication\Poor	No	4.69%	1	1
Nodes\\Themes\\Executive Involvement - Integration Planning	Yes	29.94%	0	1
Nodes\\Themes\\Executive Involvement - Integration Planning\Comprehensive	No	29.94%	1	1
Nodes\\Themes\\Human Capital Management\Human Capital Management - Comprehensive	No	29.94%	1	1
Nodes\\Themes\\Organizational Culture Integration Preparation	No	5.35%	1	1
Nodes\\Themes\\Organizational Culture Integration Preparation\Organizational Culture - Limited	No	5.35%	1	1
Nodes\\Themes\\Perception of Integration Preparation\Effective	No	2.72%	1	1

123

Hierarchical Name	Aggregate	Coverage	Number Of Coding	Number Of Users Coding
Cases				
Nodes\\Cases\\Participant 1	No	100.00%	1	1
Nodes\\Questions - Topical Coding Categories\\Question 2C - IP Change Management	No	10.30%	1	1
Nodes\\Questions - Topical Coding Categories\\Question 2A - IP Organizational Culture	No	33.42%	1	1
Nodes\\Questions - Topical Coding Categories\\Question 2B - IP - Human Capital Management	No	30.34%	1	1
Nodes\\Questions - Topical Coding Categories\\Question 2D(2) -	No	3.03%	1	1
Nodes\\Questions - Topical Coding Categories\\Question 3 - Percieved Effectiveness of IP	No	10.51%	1	1

Internals\\Participant 10

Node

Hierarchical Name	Aggregate	Coverage	Number Of Coding	Number Of Users Coding
Nodes\\Archive\\Participant 10	No	100.00%	1	1
Nodes\\Questions - Topical Coding Categories\\Question 1	No	9.79%	1	1
Nodes\\Questions - Topical Coding Categories\\Question 2D(1) - Simulatenously	No	12.53%	1	1
Nodes\\Themes\\Change Management Integration Planning\Change Management - Limited	No	11.66%	1	1
Nodes\\Themes\\Communication	Yes	11.66%	0	1
Nodes\\Themes\\Communication\Excellent	No	11.66%	1	1
Nodes\\Themes\\Human Capital Management\Human Capital Management - Limited	No	11.66%	1	1
Nodes\\Themes\\Organizational Culture Integration Preparation\Organizational Culture - Limited	No	31.53%	2	1
Nodes\\Themes\\Perception of Integration	No	20.35%	1	1

Cases

Hierarchical Name	Aggregate	Coverage	Number Of Coding	Number Of Users Coding
Nodes\\Cases\\Participant 10	No	100.00%	1	1
Nodes\\Questions - Topical Coding Categories\\Question 2A - IP Organizational Culture	No	19.81%	1	1
Nodes\\Questions - Topical Coding Categories\\Question 2B - IP - Human Capital Management	No	22.87%	1	1
Nodes\\Questions - Topical Coding Categories\\Question 3 - Percieved Effectiveness of IP	No	20.30%	1	1

Internals\\Participant 11

Node

Hierarchical Name	Aggregate	Coverage	Number Of Coding	Number Of Users Coding
Nodes\\Archive\\Participant 11	No	100.00%	1	1
Nodes\\Questions - Topical Coding Categories\\Question 1	No	24.58%	1	1
Nodes\\Themes\\Change Management Integration Planning\Change Management - Comprehensive	No	29.49%	2	1
Nodes\\Themes\\Communication	Yes	18.91%	0	1
Nodes\\Themes\\Communication\Excellent	No	18.91%	1	1
Nodes\\Themes\\Executive Involvement - Integration Planning	Yes	29.49%	0	1
Nodes\\Themes\\Executive Involvement - Integration Planning\Comprehensive	No	29.49%	2	1
Nodes\\Themes\\Human Capital Management\Human Capital Management - Comprehensive	No	10.58%	1	1
Nodes\\Themes\\Integration Project Team	No	44.36%	1	1
Nodes\\Themes\\Integration Project Team\Benefits	No	10.58%	1	1
Nodes\\Themes\\Integration Project Team\Compensation	No	10.58%	1	1
Nodes\\Themes\\Integration Project Team\Legal	No	10.58%	1	1
Nodes\\Themes\\Integration Project Team\Organizational	No	10.58%	1	1
Nodes\\Themes\\Integration Project Team\Talent	No	10.58%	1	1
Nodes\\Themes\\Organizational Culture Integration Preparation\Organizational Culture - Comprehensive	No	10.58%	1	1
Nodes\\Themes\\Perception of Integration Preparation\Effective	No	18.91%	1	1

Cases

Hierarchical Name	Aggregate	Coverage	Number Of Coding	Number Of Users Coding
Nodes\\Cases\\Participant 11	No	100.00%	1	1
Nodes\\Questions - Topical Coding Categories\\Question 2A - IP Organizational Culture	No	9.29%	1	1
Nodes\\Questions - Topical Coding Categories\\Question 2B - IP - Human Capital Management	No	16.63%	1	1
Nodes\\Questions - Topical Coding Categories\\Question 2D(2) -	No	16.45%	1	1

Internals\\Participant 12

Node

Hierarchical Name	Aggregate	Coverage	Number Of Coding	Number Of Users Coding
Nodes\\Archive\\Participant 12	No	100.00%	1	1
Nodes\\Questions - Topical Coding Categories\\Question 1	No	1.19%	1	1
Nodes\\Questions - Topical Coding Categories\\Question 2D(1) - Simulatenously	No	11.12%	1	1
Nodes\\Themes\\Change Management Integration Planning\Change Management - Comprehensive	No	12.58%	1	1
Nodes\\Themes\\Communication	Yes	32.41%	0	1

Hierarchical Name	Aggregate	Coverage	Number Of Coding	Number Of Users Coding
Nodes\\Themes\\Communication\Excellent	No	32.41%	1	1
Nodes\\Themes\\Executive Involvement - Integration Planning	Yes	32.41%	0	1
Nodes\\Themes\\Executive Involvement - Integration Planning\Comprehensive	No	32.41%	1	1
Nodes\\Themes\\Human Capital Management\Human Capital Management - Comprehensive	No	32.41%	1	1
Nodes\\Themes\\Integration Project Team	No	4.20%	1	1
Nodes\\Themes\\Organizational Culture Integration Preparation\Organizational Culture - Comprehensive	No	16.68%	1	1
Nodes\\Themes\\Perception of Integration Preparation\Effective	No	13.33%	1	1

Cases

Nodes\\Cases\\Participant 12	No	100.00%	1	1
Nodes\\Questions - Topical Coding Categories\\Question 2C - IP Change Management	No	12.60%	1	1
Nodes\\Questions - Topical Coding Categories\\Question 2A - IP Organizational Culture	No	16.64%	1	1
Nodes\\Questions - Topical Coding Categories\\Question 2B - IP - Human Capital Management	No	36.61%	1	1

Internals\\Participant 13

Node

Nodes\\Archive\\Participant 13	No	100.00%	1	1
Nodes\\Questions - Topical Coding Categories\\Question 1	No	5.97%	1	1
Nodes\\Themes\\Change Management Integration Planning\Change Management - Limited	No	12.84%	1	1
Nodes\\Themes\\Communication	Yes	16.91%	0	1
Nodes\\Themes\\Communication\Excellent	No	16.91%	1	1
Nodes\\Themes\\Executive Involvement - Integration Planning	Yes	20.08%	0	1
Nodes\\Themes\\Executive Involvement - Integration	No	20.08%	1	1
Nodes\\Themes\\Human Capital Management\Human Capital Management - Limited	No	20.08%	1	1
Nodes\\Themes\\Perception of Integration Preparation\Effective	No	12.80%	1	1

Cases

Nodes\\Cases\\Participant 13	No	100.00%	1	1
Nodes\\Questions - Topical Coding Categories\\Question 2D(2) -	No	18.67%	1	1

Hierarchical Name	Aggregate	Coverage	Number Of Coding	Number Of Users Coding
Node				
Nodes\\Archive\\Participant 2	No	100.00%	1	1
Nodes\\Questions - Topical Coding Categories\\Question 1	No	3.12%	1	1
Nodes\\Questions - Topical Coding Categories\\Question 2D(1) - Simulatenously	No	9.16%	1	1
Nodes\\Themes\\Change Management Integration Planning\Change Management - Comprehensive	No	16.99%	1	1
Nodes\\Themes\\Communication	Yes	16.99%	0	1
Nodes\\Themes\\Communication\Excellent	No	16.99%	1	1
Nodes\\Themes\\Executive Involvement - Integration Planning	Yes	40.44%	0	1
Nodes\\Themes\\Executive Involvement - Integration Planning\Comprehensive	No	40.44%	1	1
Nodes\\Themes\\Human Capital Management\Human Capital Management - Limited	No	23.44%	1	1
Nodes\\Themes\\Integration Project Team\Organizational	No	30.84%	2	1
Nodes\\Themes\\Integration Project Team\Talent	No	32.61%	2	1
Nodes\\Themes\\Organizational Culture Integration Preparation\Organizational Culture - Comprehensive	No	21.68%	1	1
Nodes\\Themes\\Perception of Integration Preparation\Effective	No	6.22%	1	1
Cases				
Nodes\\Cases\\Participant 2	No	100.00%	1	1
Nodes\\Questions - Topical Coding Categories\\Question 2C - IP Change Management	No	16.94%	1	1
Nodes\\Questions - Topical Coding Categories\\Question 2A - IP Organizational Culture	No	21.68%	1	1
Nodes\\Questions - Topical Coding Categories\\Question 2B - IP - Human Capital Management	No	23.39%	1	1
Nodes\\Questions - Topical Coding Categories\\Question 3 - Percieved Effectiveness of IP	No	15.23%	1	1
Node				
Nodes\\Archive\\Participant 3	No	100.00%	1	1
Nodes\\HR Integration Preparation - Yes and No Completed	No	0.50%	1	1
Nodes\\Questions - Topical Coding Categories\\Question 1	No	7.45%	1	1
Nodes\\Themes\\Change Management Integration Planning\Change Management - Limited	No	19.81%	1	1
Nodes\\Themes\\Communication	Yes	41.63%	0	1
Nodes\\Themes\\Communication\Poor	No	41.63%	2	1

Hierarchical Name	Aggregate	Coverage	Number Of Coding	Number Of Users Coding
Nodes\\Themes\\Executive Involvement - Integration Planning	Yes	7.00%	0	1
Nodes\\Themes\\Executive Involvement - Integration Planning\Comprehensive	No	7.00%	1	1
Nodes\\Themes\\Human Capital Management\Human Capital Management - Limited	No	34.63%	1	1
Nodes\\Themes\\Organizational Culture Integration Preparation\Organizational Culture - Limited	No	34.63%	1	1
Nodes\\Themes\\Perception of Integration	No	61.45%	3	1

Cases

Nodes\\Cases\\Participant 3	No	100.00%	1	1
Nodes\\Questions - Topical Coding Categories\\Question 2C - IP Change Management	No	9.81%	1	1
Nodes\\Questions - Topical Coding Categories\\Question 2A - IP Organizational Culture	No	12.18%	1	1
Nodes\\Questions - Topical Coding Categories\\Question 2B - IP - Human Capital Management	No	18.54%	2	1
Nodes\\Questions - Topical Coding Categories\\Question 2D(2) -	No	2.04%	1	1
Nodes\\Questions - Topical Coding Categories\\Question 3 - Percieved Effectiveness of IP	No	33.45%	2	1

Internals\\Participant 4

Node

Nodes\\Questions - Topical Coding Categories\\Question 1	No	0.15%	1	1
Nodes\\Questions - Topical Coding Categories\\Question 2D(1) - Simultaneously	No	9.60%	1	1
Nodes\\Themes\\Change Management Integration Planning\Change Management - Comprehensive	No	46.46%	2	1
Nodes\\Themes\\Communication	Yes	34.86%	0	1
Nodes\\Themes\\Communication\Excellent	No	34.86%	1	1
Nodes\\Themes\\Executive Involvement - Integration Planning	Yes	44.60%	0	1
Nodes\\Themes\\Executive Involvement - Integration Planning\Comprehensive	No	44.60%	1	1
Nodes\\Themes\\Human Capital Management\Human Capital Management - Comprehensive	No	34.86%	1	1
Nodes\\Themes\\Integration Project Team\Benefits	No	34.86%	1	1
Nodes\\Themes\\Integration Project Team\Compensation	No	34.86%	1	1
Nodes\\Themes\\Integration Project Team\Talent	No	44.60%	1	1
Nodes\\Themes\\Organizational Culture Integration Preparation\Organizational Culture - Comprehensive	No	21.62%	1	1
Nodes\\Themes\\Perception of Integration Preparation\Effective	No	11.59%	1	1

Hierarchical Name	Aggregate	Coverage	Number Of Coding	Number Of Users Coding
Cases				
Nodes\\Cases\\Participant 4	No	100.00%	1	1
Nodes\\Questions - Topical Coding Categories\\Question 2C - IP Change Management	No	6.07%	1	1
Nodes\\Questions - Topical Coding Categories\\Question 2A - IP Organizational Culture	No	21.62%	1	1
Nodes\\Questions - Topical Coding Categories\\Question 2B - IP - Human Capital Management	No	44.60%	1	1
Nodes\\Questions - Topical Coding Categories\\Question 3 - Percieved Effectiveness of IP	No	5.52%	1	1

Internals\\Participant 5

Node

Hierarchical Name	Aggregate	Coverage	Number Of Coding	Number Of Users Coding
Nodes\\Questions - Topical Coding Categories\\Question 1	No	2.21%	1	1
Nodes\\Themes\\Communication	Yes	16.18%	0	1
Nodes\\Themes\\Communication\Excellent	No	6.29%	1	1
Nodes\\Themes\\Communication\Poor	No	9.89%	1	1
Nodes\\Themes\\Executive Involvement - Integration Planning	Yes	14.03%	0	1
Nodes\\Themes\\Executive Involvement - Integration Planning\Comprehensive	No	14.03%	1	1
Nodes\\Themes\\Human Capital Management\Human Capital Management - Comprehensive	No	14.03%	1	1
Nodes\\Themes\\Integration Project Team\Benefits	No	12.93%	1	1
Nodes\\Themes\\Integration Project Team\Compensation	No	12.93%	1	1
Nodes\\Themes\\Integration Project Team\Organizational	No	12.93%	1	1
Nodes\\Themes\\Integration Project Team\Talent	No	12.93%	1	1
Nodes\\Themes\\Perception of Integration Preparation\Effective	No	20.68%	1	1

Cases

Hierarchical Name	Aggregate	Coverage	Number Of Coding	Number Of Users Coding
Nodes\\Cases\\Participant 5	No	100.00%	1	1
Nodes\\Questions - Topical Coding Categories\\Question 2A - IP Organizational Culture	No	5.76%	1	1
Nodes\\Questions - Topical Coding Categories\\Question 2B - IP - Human Capital Management	No	65.06%	2	1
Nodes\\Questions - Topical Coding Categories\\Question 3 - Percieved Effectiveness of IP	No	20.68%	1	1

Hierarchical Name	Aggregate Coverage	Number Of Coding	Number Of Users Coding
Internals\\Participant 6			
Node			
Nodes\\Questions - Topical Coding Categories\\Question 1	No	1.34%	1	1
Nodes\\Themes\\Change Management Integration Planning\Change Management - Comprehensive	No	21.91%	1	1
Nodes\\Themes\\Communication	Yes	21.91%	0	1
Nodes\\Themes\\Communication\Excellent	No	21.91%	1	1
Nodes\\Themes\\Executive Involvement - Integration Planning	Yes	21.91%	0	1
Nodes\\Themes\\Executive Involvement - Integration Planning\Comprehensive	No	21.91%	1	1
Nodes\\Themes\\Human Capital Management\Human Capital Management - Comprehensive	No	28.86%	1	1
Nodes\\Themes\\Integration Project Team\Benefits	No	28.86%	1	1
Nodes\\Themes\\Integration Project Team\Compensation	No	28.86%	1	1
Nodes\\Themes\\Integration Project Team\Legal	No	28.86%	1	1
Nodes\\Themes\\Integration Project Team\Organizational	No	28.86%	1	1
Nodes\\Themes\\Integration Project Team\Talent	No	28.86%	1	1
Nodes\\Themes\\Perception of Integration Preparation\Effective	No	11.45%	1	1
Cases			
Nodes\\Cases\\Participant 6	No	100.00%	1	1
Nodes\\Questions - Topical Coding Categories\\Question 2C - IP Change Management	No	35.24%	2	1
Nodes\\Questions - Topical Coding Categories\\Question 2B - IP - Human Capital Management	No	25.17%	1	1
Nodes\\Questions - Topical Coding Categories\\Question 2D(2) -	No	8.85%	1	1
Nodes\\Questions - Topical Coding Categories\\Question 3 - Percieved Effectiveness of IP	No	11.76%	1	1
Internals\\Participant 7			
Node			
Nodes\\Questions - Topical Coding Categories\\Question 1	No	0.20%	1	1
Nodes\\Themes\\Change Management Integration Planning\Change Management - Comprehensive	No	28.03%	1	1
Nodes\\Themes\\Communication	Yes	28.03%	0	1
Nodes\\Themes\\Communication\Excellent	No	28.03%	1	1
Nodes\\Themes\\Executive Involvement - Integration Planning	Yes	38.88%	0	1
Nodes\\Themes\\Executive Involvement - Integration Planning\Comprehensive	No	10.84%	1	1
Nodes\\Themes\\Executive Involvement - Integration	No	28.03%	1	1

Hierarchical Name	Aggregate	Coverage	Number Of Coding	Number Of Users Coding
Nodes\\Themes\\Human Capital Management\Human Capital Management - Comprehensive	No	28.03%	1	1
Nodes\\Themes\\Integration Project Team	No	10.84%	1	1
Nodes\\Themes\\Integration Project Team\Benefits	No	11.17%	1	1
Nodes\\Themes\\Integration Project Team\Compensation	No	11.17%	1	1
Nodes\\Themes\\Integration Project Team\Legal	No	11.17%	1	1
Nodes\\Themes\\Integration Project Team\Organizational	No	11.17%	1	1
Nodes\\Themes\\Integration Project Team\Talent	No	11.17%	1	1
Nodes\\Themes\\Organizational Culture Integration Preparation\Organizational Culture - Comprehensive	No	16.82%	1	1
Nodes\\Themes\\Perception of Integration Preparation\Effective	No	14.65%	1	1

Cases

Nodes\\Cases\\Participant 7	No	100.00%	1	1
Nodes\\Questions - Topical Coding Categories\\Question 2A - IP Organizational Culture	No	21.69%	1	1

Internals\\Participant 8

Node

Nodes\\Questions - Topical Coding Categories\\Question 1	No	1.48%	1	1
Nodes\\Themes\\Change Management Integration Planning\Change Management - Comprehensive	No	14.68%	1	1
Nodes\\Themes\\Communication	Yes	14.68%	0	1
Nodes\\Themes\\Communication\Excellent	No	14.68%	1	1
Nodes\\Themes\\Executive Involvement - Integration Planning	Yes	30.19%	0	1
Nodes\\Themes\\Executive Involvement - Integration Planning\Comprehensive	No	30.19%	1	1
Nodes\\Themes\\Human Capital Management\Human Capital Management - Comprehensive	No	13.62%	1	1
Nodes\\Themes\\Integration Project Team	No	6.53%	1	1
Nodes\\Themes\\Integration Project Team\Benefits	No	13.62%	1	1
Nodes\\Themes\\Integration Project Team\Compensation	No	13.62%	1	1
Nodes\\Themes\\Integration Project Team\Organizational	No	16.57%	1	1
Nodes\\Themes\\Integration Project Team\Talent	No	13.62%	1	1
Nodes\\Themes\\Organizational Culture Integration Preparation\Organizational Culture - Comprehensive	No	16.57%	1	1
Nodes\\Themes\\Perception of Integration Preparation\Effective	No	19.67%	1	1

Cases

Nodes\\Cases\\Participant 8	No	100.00%	1	1

Hierarchical Name	Aggregate	Coverage	Number Of Coding	Number Of Users Coding
Nodes\\Questions - Topical Coding Categories\\Question 2C - IP Change Management	No	14.64%	1	1
Nodes\\Questions - Topical Coding Categories\\Question 2A - IP Organizational Culture	No	32.04%	1	1
Nodes\\Questions - Topical Coding Categories\\Question 2B - IP - Human Capital Management	No	13.62%	1	1
Nodes\\Questions - Topical Coding Categories\\Question 2D(2) -	No	10.77%	1	1
Nodes\\Questions - Topical Coding Categories\\Question 3 - Percieved Effectiveness of IP	No	19.67%	1	1

Internals\\Participant 9

Node

Nodes\\Archive\\Participant 9	No	100.00%	1	1
Nodes\\Questions - Topical Coding Categories\\Question 1	No	12.63%	1	1
Nodes\\Questions - Topical Coding Categories\\Question 2D(1) - Simultatenously	No	12.50%	1	1
Nodes\\Themes\\Executive Involvement - Integration Planning	Yes	25.89%	0	1
Nodes\\Themes\\Executive Involvement - Integration Planning\Comprehensive	No	25.89%	1	1
Nodes\\Themes\\Human Capital Management\Human Capital Management - Comprehensive	No	25.89%	1	1
Nodes\\Themes\\Integration Project Team\Benefits	No	38.39%	1	1
Nodes\\Themes\\Integration Project Team\Compensation	No	38.39%	1	1
Nodes\\Themes\\Integration Project Team\Organizational	No	23.28%	2	1
Nodes\\Themes\\Integration Project Team\Talent	No	38.39%	1	1
Nodes\\Themes\\Organizational Culture Integration Preparation\Organizational Culture - Comprehensive	No	10.78%	1	1
Nodes\\Themes\\Perception of Integration Preparation\Effective	No	16.13%	1	1

Cases

Nodes\\Cases\\Participant 9	No	100.00%	1	1
Nodes\\Questions - Topical Coding Categories\\Question 2A - IP Organizational Culture	No	19.64%	1	1
Nodes\\Questions - Topical Coding Categories\\Question 2B - IP - Human Capital Management	No	25.82%	1	1
Nodes\\Questions - Topical Coding Categories\\Question 3 - Percieved Effectiveness of IP	No	16.20%	1	1

CPSIA information can be obtained
at www.ICGtesting.com
Printed in the USA
LVIW021223040113

314389LV00007B